# ALL CHILDREN SUCCESSFUL

# ALL CHILDREN SUCCESSFUL

## real answers for helping at-risk elementary students

VITO GERMINARIO, Ed.D.
JANET CERVALLI, M.A.
EVELYN HUNT OGDEN, Ed.D.

**TECHNOMIC**
PUBLISHING CO., INC.

Lancaster · Basel

# All Children Successful
a **TECHNOMIC**® publication

*Published in the Western Hemisphere by*
Technomic Publishing Company, Inc.
851 New Holland Avenue
Box 3535
Lancaster, Pennsylvania 17604 U.S.A.

*Distributed in the Rest of the World by*
Technomic Publishing AG

Printed in the United States of America
10  9  8  7  6  5  4  3  2

Main entry under title:
    All Children Successful: Real Answers for Helping At-Risk Elementary Students

A Technomic Publishing Company book
Bibliography: p. 197

Library of Congress Card No. 92-53827
ISBN No. 0-87762-921-8

*To Anna and Sergio Germinario, my mother and father who have been a*
*constant source of love, inspiration, and support.*

Vito Germinario

*To my Hiltonia friends.*

Evelyn Hunt Ogden

*To my father, Thomas, and to all the children in my life,*
*especially Michael and Matthew.*

Janet Cervalli

# CONTENTS

THE MOORESTOWN AND East Brunswick Public School systems and the members of their Student Assistance Teams who participated in the development and implementation of programs to assist students at risk.

Ellen J. Andreas for her friendship and assistance in typing portions of the manuscript.

Diana Robinson who spent many hours editing and making recommendations to improve the work.

To all of them our warmest thanks!

ALL ELEMENTARY SCHOOL age children are at times students at risk, and within every school there is a portion of the student body that consistently shows a lack of the necessary intellectual, emotional, and/or social skills to take full advantage of the educational opportunities available to them. Often these children become disaffected and openly or passively reject school—they are students at risk.

The purpose of the school is to maximize learning for all children. The most obvious way in which schools attempt to accomplish their mission is through direct instruction in the curriculum areas. However, an additional way to maximize learning is to minimize the effects of those factors that limit the potential of children. The climate of the school and classroom, the prevention and intervention strategies used, and a commitment to excellence that exceeds academic standards can exert powerful effects on minimizing risk and maximizing learning.

There are several reasons why teachers and administrators should be increasingly concerned with understanding and managing the factors that place limits on learning.

The first reason for concern is the question of equity in access to education. As laws and policies have been implemented to educate the disabled child, the bilingual child, the gifted child, etc., so it can be argued that the disaffected students, the majority of whom have normal intelligence, require special programs or strategies to truly benefit from their educational experience. Interventions at an early age may reduce or eliminate the need for more complex interventions in later years.

A second reason is that societal expectations for schools have changed concerning issues that were traditionally addressed within the family. The reality is that schools have little choice but to embrace these new expectations. The parents of at least 40 percent of the children born this year will divorce. One in four girls will become pregnant during her high school years. Only one in one thousand college freshman women plans a career as a homemaker. The family has changed, society has changed and the role of the school has changed.

Increasingly, parents look to schools for help. Their first concern is the provision of a secure environment for their children. But more importantly, schools are asked to assume a direct role in the teaching of essential life skills that were traditionally within the domain of family and church.

A third reason is that disaffected or at-risk students have potentially negative effects on the attitudes, behaviors, and achievements of other students, teachers, and administrators.

It is our hope that this book will assist teachers, principals, central administrators, and boards of education to develop elementary/middle school programs and classroom strategies to maximize the learning opportunities for at-risk students. Specifically this book will address a wide variety of philosophical, sociological, and instructional phenomena that will help establish a climate for identifying and assisting at-risk children.

It should be noted that this book will only deal with those skills and activities that are within the normal reach and educational background of school staff. Thus, concepts related to effective schools and effective teacher research will serve as the basic framework from which any strategies or programs should evolve.

Although many prevention and intervention techniques are discussed in this book, we believe that the role of the school staff is not that of therapists! Most of the problems or learning distractors discussed in this book can be addressed by the day-to-day actions of the school staff in their interaction with students in the classroom. In such cases as addiction, attempted suicide, child abuse, or other major dysfunctional behavior, the role of the school should be to identify and refer the child to outside experts.

It is important to understand that programs aimed at assuring student wellness need to be carefully articulated throughout a child's educational experience. A comprehensive plan makes it possible for schools to take advantage of the accumulated learning, attitudes, and behaviors developed in previous grades. Further, it provides a stable environment to promote specific teaching behaviors aimed at maintaining a positive class climate and the teaching and reinforcing of needed life skills. Just as a good curriculum is aligned to ensure sequential presentation of content, so a conscientious program to enrich the learning environment must be designed to service students in a systematic, consistent manner throughout their school experience.

This book is guided by several basic premises that will provide focus to those educators who are committed to educating at-risk students. Administrators and teachers can:

- Identify situations that are risks to learning and opportunities to enhance learning.
- Implement programs that will maximize the climate for learning.
- Prepare for the periodic crises facing children in their schools and classrooms and minimize the negative effects of such problems.
- Teach students behaviors and skills that promote further learning and reduce the chances of involvement in destructive behavior.
- Improve student achievement by more systematically applying what is known about educating children.

To facilitate its use, this book has been organized into four sections. Part One deals with the role of the school, the teacher, the principal, the central administration, and the school board in promoting learning for all students as well as those who are at-risk. Part Two provides guidelines and procedures for the development of a comprehensive student assistance program. Part Three provides strategies, interventions, and case studies related to specific at-risk situations. Part Four addresses planning, reporting, and evaluation of student assistance programs.

This book is designed to serve as a guide to promoting student well-being and learning. Further, the organization of the book provides a practical framework by which specific high-risk student behaviors can be addressed. Finally, this book can serve as a desk reference that provides specific guidelines, procedures, and correspondence needed to plan effectively a total student assistance program or to respond to the variety of crisis situations confronting staff in schools today.

# PART ONE

# THE ROLE OF THE SCHOOL IN PROMOTING LEARNING FOR THE AT-RISK STUDENT

# CHAPTER 1

# The At-Risk Elementary School Student

THE PURPOSE OF the elementary school is to promote learning. To achieve this purpose the school must deliver a well-defined and appropriate curriculum. In addition, the school must strive to develop an environment that maximizes learning and minimizes conditions that interfere with learning. The degree to which the school accomplishes these objectives is the measure of its degree of "wellness."

A "well" student is defined as one who is achieving at a rate commensurate with his or her ability; has a positive attitude toward self, teachers, and school; has positive relationships with peers; and does not exhibit destructive behaviors. A "well" school is one that has addressed the learning environment of the school and has taken action to reduce or eliminate impediments to learning. It is a school, therefore, in which students of all types are achieving academically. This means there is a positive attitude toward school and staff, high expectations, and freedom from destructive behaviors in the school environment. Since school is only part of a student's or a teacher's or an administrator's life, the school does not control all the variables that affect wellness. Therefore, schools cannot be totally well in terms of learning at all times. However, principals, teachers, counselors, and support staff can have profound effects on the degree of wellness of the school and students individually. It is a matter of choice within a continuum.

This chapter will address the nature of risk of elementary students. Additionally, rationale and strategies for a comprehensive program of prevention and intervention will be presented.

## THE NATURE OF RISK

All children are, at times, at risk of failure. Yet, most can effectively utilize the standard resources and support systems established at home or school to deal with the trials and tribulations of growing up. As a result

3

of their positive developmental experiences they emerge as young adults satisfied with who they are and pleased with the approval and pride from their families and friends. Similarly, children who achieve in school experience success and, typically, develop positive attitudes toward school and themselves.

Unfortunately, there is a portion of every school population that consistently shows a lack of necessary intellectual, emotional, and/or social skills to take full advantage of the educational opportunities available to them. Often, these students become disenchanted and, ultimately, passively or openly reject school. It's these students who are at high risk of failure.

There is no prototype at-risk elementary school student. Students who do not succeed in our schools come from all social, ethnic, and racial groups. Yet, various demographic characteristics tend to place certain students at a potentially higher risk for school failure.

Certain key demographic factors have been found to be more closely related to at-risk status. Pallas, Natriello, and McDill (1989) characterize the educationally disadvantaged child as one who has been exposed to certain background factors or experiences in formal schooling, family, or community. Although not a categorical model to predict at-risk status, these authors have determined that particular combinations of risk factors have been shown to be particularly detrimental to success. Examples of these are single-parent homes with low incomes and parents with limited English proficiency who have no high school diploma. Similarly, a study conducted by the National Center for Education Statistics (U.S. Department of Education, 1988) identifies indicators of at-risk status. These include (among others), living in a single-parent family, low parental income and/or education, limited English proficiency, having a brother or sister who dropped out of high school, and being at home alone without an adult for a period greater than three hours on weekdays.

Although helpful in a general sense, demographic characteristics, in and of themselves, can not consistently identify those elementary school students destined for school failure. An examination of characteristics and school behaviors of at-risk students can further help identify which children are at greatest risk for failure. Research has shown that the characteristics listed below are closely associated with school failure:

- attendance problems
- previous school retention

- prior school suspensions
- working two or more years below grade level
- lack of participation in extracurricular activities
- special program placement

From both an empirical and common sense perspective, these behaviors can accurately identify those students who, for whatever reason, will not meet with school success. Yet, these characteristics tend to manifest themselves long after a student has begun to develop attitude and behavioral patterns that lead to school failure. Instead, it may be more beneficial to examine general descriptors of a student's profile to establish parameters for determining the nature of risk. A review of the research can help synthesize this profile by analyzing four basic conditions—self-concept, alienation, lack of school success, and student learning style.

## STUDENT SELF-CONCEPT

Self-concept has been found to be related to students' grades, test scores, and other significant educational outcomes (Coleman et al., 1966). Teachers instinctively know that when students feel better about themselves, they tend to do better in school. It becomes critical that school personnel actively seek ways of promoting self-esteem in the classroom and of promoting a school climate that conscientiously attempts to foster students' feelings of pride in themselves and their schools.

### Alienation

For at-risk students, lack of success in school both contributes to and results from an increased sense of alienation from school as an institution. Newman (1981) associates alienation in schools with disruptive student behaviors and poor achievement. He suggests that student disengagement generally goes unrecognized as the source of many school problems. He insists that reducing student alienation is key to engaging students in the positive benefits in their schooling.

Thus, schools need to identify and revise school and classroom practices that send negative messages about school membership and belonging. Common practices associated with class grouping patterns, discipline and attendance policies, school regulations, school curriculum, school rules, and special class placement may be rooted in good intentions; yet they may, in fact, lead to increased feelings of isolation and lack of belonging.

### *Level of School Success*

Success in early years is a critical prerequisite to success in later schooling and, ultimately, in life. Third graders who are reading a year or more below grade level or who have been retained one or more times are particularly at risk, and when these students are from low socioeconomic backgrounds and attend school with many other poor children, their chances of eventually graduating from high school approach zero (McPartland and Shores, 1990). School failure leads to messages of rejection and poor sense of self. Without basic academic and social skills, children face failure every day and may quickly reach the conclusion that they are incapable and that schools don't care about their learning.

Success, however, can come from a variety of aspects of school life. Achievement, not only in academics, but in areas related to athletics or aesthetics can lead to increased feelings of self with a greater sense of belonging to the mainstream of the school. It becomes imperative that schools continue to examine how they incorporate a success orientation in daily practices. Clearly, teachers have the greatest impact on the sense of success a student may encounter. Yet, the principal, coach, also play director, custodian, and bus driver provide significant contributions to the at-risk student's feeling of belonging and worth.

## LEARNING STYLE

Every student has a preferred learning style. While most students can learn through a variety of sensory stimuli and within different learning environments, enough research is available to support the notion that teaching through learning styles can improve student learning (Dunn and Dunn, et al.).

Learning style is comprised of a combination of environmental, emotional, sociological, and psychological elements that permit individuals to receive, store, and use knowledge or abilities (Dunn and Dunn, 1983).

There is some evidence to suggest that at-risk students may have measurably different learning styles. In fact, at-risk students may have predominant learning modalities that differ significantly from traditional teaching styles. In a recent study, at-risk learners were identified as having poor to fair auditory and visual learning capabilities. However, a very large percentage of these students demonstrated high preference for tactical and kinesthetic learning experiences.

It becomes important then, that we begin to train teachers to utilize a more multi-sensory approach with identified at-risk students. It seems logical that providing variability in instructional delivery systems would ultimately help all learners.

## PROGRAM RATIONALE

Schools have an expressed obligation to educate all students. This responsibility is most typically met through direct instruction in the traditional curriculum areas. However, schools must now embrace the responsibility of successfully educating those students who, for whatever reason, come to school unable to maximize their learning potential. No longer can schools afford to disregard the role that society has placed upon them.

There are a variety of factors that compel our schools to engage in early prevention and intervention initiatives to help ensure the success of our elementary school students.

The first is that a variety of societal problems are, at least in part, the result of a poor education. Early success in school correlates with high school graduation. More than 80 percent of prison inmates are high school dropouts, (U.S. Department of Education, 1990). The best way to reduce crime is to increase education, because the chances are greater that a high school dropout will go to prison than they are that a smoker will contract cancer (Hodghenson, 1990).

The second concern is the question of equity in access to educational opportunity. State and federal laws have been enacted to help educate learning disabled children, non-English speaking children, gifted children, etc.; so it can be argued that the disaffected students, the majority of whom have normal intelligence, require specialized learning experiences and support systems to truly maximize their learning potential.

A third reason is linked to changing societal expectations for our schools. The world has become increasingly complex for the elementary school students. Confronted with increased pressure from familial, environmental, and social stresses, today's youngsters may have greater difficulty determining their places in the world. Increasingly, parents will look to the school for help. Schools have now been asked to assume a more direct role in teaching essential life skills that were traditionally within the domain of family and church.

Finally, schools have the awesome responsibility of preparing students for the roles they will be asked to play in our ever complex society. It is through our efforts that a significant foundation can be established to ensure success for a generation of young Americans.

## COMPONENTS OF A COMPREHENSIVE PROGRAM

Because the factors that place a student at risk are numerous and complex, successful programming for at-risk students must address multiple needs and be carefully tailored to meet the individuals they serve. Nonetheless, general parameters of effective programs emerge, which can be identified.

Successful programs in elementary schools are comprehensive and intensive. They start with a viable mechanism to identify at-risk students and provide the systematic application of instructional strategies and school programs that (1) help students succeed in school, (2) help students overcome feelings of isolation and alienation, and (3) optimally, create an environment that formulates self-motivation and student interest in continued learning.

Specifically, successful programs:

- Develop a curriculum basis for school improvement initiatives. Teachers are trained best to teach. Programs that are rooted in counseling or the dynamics of the family are best suited for psychologists and social workers. Schools must capitalize on the staff's ability to improve student learning and self-esteem as the most primary of all at-risk prevention vehicles. Providing a success orientation for elementary school students will significantly increase the chances of life-long success.
- Stress intimacy and individual attention. Virtually all successful programs provide for strong personal attention to each student. They strive to create a feeling of nurturing and belonging that is often absent from the home and school experience of at-risk students.
- Deal with the child as part of the family and the family as part of the neighborhood. Research clearly shows that student attitudes and performance are better when parents are

supportive and involved in the school environment (National School Boards Association, 1988). Special care should be given to accommodate access to the school for the parents of at-risk students. Parenting classes, home visits, and a recognition of parental responsibilities in educating their children are examples of bringing parents into the mainstream of school life.

- Utilize a team approach to programming for the at-risk student. The responsibility cannot fall on the counselor, child psychologist, nurse, or special education teacher. The entire school community must learn to embrace its responsibility to assist in the education of at-risk students.
- Possess caring, dedicated staff members who have the time and the skills to build relationships of trust and respect with at-risk children and their families. Thus, the school must make a commitment to training the staff as to the nature of risk and in strategies that facilitate the learning of the at-risk student.
- Monitor program. Very few programs fail because of lack of initial enthusiasm or the utility of purpose. Instead, many programs fail because they are either not implemented as designed, or they are not periodically assessed for their impact on the intended outcome.
- Have administrative and school board support. Through the development of policies, or commitment to provide needed resources and, most importantly, effective leadership, programs aimed at providing success for at-risk students (like all other programs) will prove beneficial.
- Evaluate program. Once implemented, monitoring must be initiated to ensure that activities are being conducted according to plan. Evaluation mechanisms must be put into place to determine if expectations/objectives are being met.

## SUMMARY

This chapter was aimed at providing a basic understanding of the nature of risk in elementary school students. Additionally, it provided the rationale and critical need for establishing comprehensive programs expressly directed toward the effective education of at-risk elementary school students.

It is upon the basic premises established above that the instructional and programmatic considerations for any attempt at educating all students, and most importantly at-risk students, should be founded.

# CHAPTER 2

# Promoting Student Well-Being — The Role of the Teacher

MOST STUDENTS ENTER school enthusiastic about the possibilities that exist for them within the school. While some have early separation or adjustment problems, most children look forward to going to school, learning new skills, and meeting new friends. However, there is considerable evidence to support the fact that feelings of school failure and symptoms of dysfunctional behavior can be identified as early as kindergarten. In extreme cases, such students become school-phobic and actively resist the formal efforts of school personnel. In other cases, the symptoms are mild, yet significant enough to interfere with their ability to maximize their learning potential. Lack of success and a sense of belonging can be major contributors to dysfunctional behavior. Yet, poor health, perceived attitudes of teachers, unstable peer relationships, and the dynamics of the home can all add to high-risk behavior (Ogden and Germinario, 1988).

Teachers and, more specifically, the climate they are able to develop in the class, have a significant impact on student success in the classroom. Similarly, the quality of teaching strategies employed and the diversity of instructional delivery systems can have a profound impression on learning and emotional outcomes. It becomes exceedingly important that teachers systematically apply instructional strategies that can be supported both in an empirical and common sense perspective that foster student achievement and well-being. The success of the efforts of elementary school teachers will have lasting impact on learning and the life-long success of their students.

Ultimately, only when more effective ways of delivering high-quality instruction are instituted in the nation's schools can we truly optimize the impact of schooling. Similarly, it is only when teachers become familiar with general instructional concepts and specific instructional strategies that we can hope to better educate our at-risk students.

This chapter will present a variety of instructional strategies aimed at developing a positive learning environment for all students. Additionally, a model for identifying at-risk students will be explored. Throughout this development, specific focus will be given to classroom practices that improve achievement for at-risk children.

## IDENTIFYING HIGH-RISK BEHAVIOR

In the previous chapter, concepts related to the general nature of risk were discussed. Although useful as a conceptual framework, attempts at identification of at-risk students early in their schooling must be initiated with behavioral guidelines that are easily observed by the teacher. These specific behaviors may include:

- students experiencing academic difficulties
- students with high absenteeism
- students with frequent complaints of illness
- students who have difficulty staying on task
- students with poor personal hygiene
- students who are isolated from peer groups
- students who are disruptive
- students who are undergoing a crisis at home such as death of a family member, divorce, separation, abuse, etc.
- students who have sudden changes in behavioral patterns

While not a categorical model to ensure the identification of all at-risk elementary-age students, sensitizing school personnel to such behaviors will increase the likelihood of early identification and intervention.

As a school intensifies its efforts to analyze high-risk student behaviors, it becomes important to systematize the collection of significant data. The development of a data collection form provides a practical framework to collect, organize, and analyze those students who have been preliminarily identified as at risk for failure (see Chapter 6 for sample form). Using such a format will help focus discussions about the child, as well as form the basis for decisions regarding the nature of risk and the appropriate intervention strategy.

As a child progresses through the grade levels, accurate information and successful approaches in dealing with his/her unique needs must be communicated. This is exceedingly important in those transitional years as a child moves from elementary to middle school, and similarly from middle school to high school. A way to systematize this process is by having the elementary teacher review each child's achievement levels and behavioral characteristics before the child moves to his/her new school.

Figure 1 is an example of how this information can be consistently gathered from school to school within a district. It is important to note that a point system like the one depicted is not aimed at developing a preestablished "cut-off" for identifying who may be at risk. Instead, it is to be used as the basis for in-depth discussions by the school personnel who will come into contact with students in those transitional grades. Thus, it becomes exceedingly important to provide the necessary time for teachers and administrators from the various sending and receiving schools to review the profile of each child so that appropriate class placement, teaching strategies, and intervention initiatives can take place. Providing a dialogue before the child enters the school will establish a framework for success from the first day.

## STRATEGIES TO PROMOTE ELEMENTARY STUDENT LEARNING AND STUDENT WELL-BEING

Quality teaching is the most primary of all at-risk prevention mechanisms. It is through the dynamics and uniqueness of student-teacher interplay that a significant portion of a child's intellectual and emotional development is achieved. Although this is admittedly difficult at times, teachers must embrace this awesome responsibility with pride and professionalism.

In its most simplistic sense, teachers engage in two primary activities: (1) establishment of the emotional and physical framework within the class, and (2) the actual delivery of instruction. This first activity, which I will characterize as *class climate*, has a profound impact upon how children feel about themselves, their teachers, and their ability to learn.

Defining class climate is not an easy task. Each one of us can remember that "special" teacher in our educational experience who, through what he/she said or how he/she acted, made a significant, lasting impression. Thus, defining that special feeling is quite difficult and will be different from student to student. Yet, for the purposes of this discussion, positive class climate will be described as a classroom where the teacher actively plans for the emotional well-being of each student. This can be characterized as having a positive feeling tone (Hunter, 1971) where a child is willing to participate without fear of failure or the risk of being excessively criticized.

## William Allen III Middle School—FIFTH GRADE

Student Name _____

| FACTOR | RATING SCALE | POINTS |
|---|---|---|
| 1. Average number of days absent grades 1–4 | 16 or more = +2 points<br>12 to 15 = +1 point<br>8 to 11 = 0 points<br>4 to 7 = −1 point<br>0 to 3 = −2 points | |
| 2. Participation in school class or other activities | None = +2 points<br>1 activity = 0 points<br>More than 1 = −2 points | |
| 3. Administrative discipline referral | 2 or more = +2 points<br>1 = +1 point<br>None = 0 points | |
| 4. Teacher's overall assessment to include students' overall adjustment to school: academic and social | Very poor = +2 points<br>Poor = +1 point<br>Average = 0 points<br>Good = −1 point<br>Excellent = −2 points | |
| 5. Counselor assessment of general characteristics (Rating assigned based on counselor's judgment) | Very poor = +2 points<br>Poor = +1 point<br>Average = 0 points<br>Good = −1 point<br>Excellent = −2 points | |
| 6. I.Q. | 91 and below = +2 points<br>92 to 100 = +1 point<br>101 to 107 = 0 points<br>108 to 115 = −1 point<br>116 and above = −2 points | |
| 7. Total reading scores (National Norms) | 1 to 50% = +2 points<br>51 to 75% = +1 point<br>76 to 80% = 0 points<br>81 to 86% = −1 point<br>87 to 99% = −2 points | |
| 8. Total math scores (National Norms) | 1 to 50% = +2 points<br>51 to 75% = +1 point<br>76 to 80% = 0 points<br>81 to 86% = −1 point<br>87 to 99% = −2 points | |
| 9. Scholastic average Grade 5 | E to D = +2 points<br>D to C− = +1 point<br>C to B = 0 points<br>B to A = −1 point<br>A = −2 points | |
| 10. Grade retention | Retained 1 yr. = +2 points | |
| | STUDENT TOTAL POINTS | |

Teacher Comments: Please feel free to provide any additional information on the back of this form for those students who you believe to be "at risk."

*Figure 1. Potential Dropout/Disaffected Student Screening Form. (Reprinted with the permission of the Moorestown Public Schools, Moorestown, New Jersey)*

## Creating a Classroom Climate for Learning

There is increasing evidence that actively planning for a positive classroom climate (as we would plan for delivery of content) can have a significant impact on student learning (Good and Brophy, 1984; Morine, 1983; Purkey and Smith, 1983).

Through a review of the research we can begin to identify those teaching skills and attitudes that promote a positive class climate. It becomes important that each teacher analyze his/her behavior as it relates to the concepts described below.

A wide range of empirical evidence leads to the conclusion that schooling affects a child's self-concept in different ways. For some children, the effects are in a positive direction; for others, the effects are often negative (Silverman, 1987).

Numerous studies have examined the relationship between academic achievement and self-concept. With few exceptions, the findings have indicated a significant and positive relationship between the two variables. To be successful in areas as important as personal and social growth requires more than isolated lessons or periodic overtures. The real growth occurs when the teacher and classroom atmosphere model and support the social concepts embodied in the lesson.

## Classrooms That Maximize Learning in Elementary Schools

Current research on teacher effectiveness forms a basis from which assessment can be made regarding the effects of teacher behavior upon a variety of measurable student outcomes. This is not to suggest the existence of a single most effective model for teaching. Instead, this research attempts to isolate specific behaviors and routines that a teacher can consciously use to improve student learning and student well-being.

While many of the findings of this research are interrelated, for discussion purposes, the information will be presented under four headings: *Climate, Planning, Instructional Management*, and *Pupil Control*.

### Class Climate

It is relatively easy to identify classrooms where a positive feeling tone exists. These feelings are typically associated with a warm, supportive environment where students are more likely to raise their hands, take an active part in the learning process, and feel more confident about the responses they anticipate receiving from the teacher when they make mistakes or need assistance in learning activities.

Recent studies have begun to identify specific climate factors that are linked in both correlation and experimental studies to increases in student learning and feelings of self-worth. Teachers must systematically analyze their behaviors as they relate to the concepts discussed below to help ensure that their behaviors and routines actively promote success for all students.

Students are likely to work better and achieve at higher levels in an atmosphere that assures that they can and will succeed in the tasks established by the teacher. This *success orientation* is especially important for the at-risk student since there is a clear relationship between achievement gains in average and below average students and the number of successful responses they give in a classroom (Brophy et al.). Thus, teachers must plan strategies and events that are designed to provide opportunities for students to get the "right answers" and thus earn the praise and reinforcement associated with high achievement. In a practical sense, teachers should look for opportunities to provide at least one successful experience each day for the at-risk student. Although difficult, the success a student receives in the classroom may be the only positive reinforcement he/she receives in a day.

Significant evidence exists (Good, 1982) to support the contention that typical elementary classrooms do not provide equal opportunity for student involvement and success. Most teachers tend to call on those students who can be consistently depended upon to provide a correct answer. This is primarily done so that: (1) a student not expected to know the answer does not get embarrassed, (2) the students in the class hear a correct and thoughtful reply, and (3) a certain degree of teacher reward becomes associated with high-quality student performances (Kerman, 1980). This phenomenon produces an interesting paradox. Students will soon realize that they are less likely to be called on; consequently, because they are not actually engaged in classroom interaction they become less able. Knowing that they probably will not be called upon, many students are likely to seek attention and success through dysfunctional means or unresponsively drift through school.

If this pattern is permitted to exist, at-risk students become increasingly less likely to gain the benefits of praise and recognition associated with success and higher levels of achievement. Interestingly, many students may become so disengaged from active learning that they actually forget how to participate. A technique to help these students is to use paired or small group learning opportunities so that the reluctant learner can begin to model successful response strategies.

As the teacher systematically increases the at-risk learner's *response opportunities*, it is very important for the teacher to analyze the amount and quality of feedback those students receive. Frequently, the majority of feedback consists of short praise, routine comment, or corrections. The ongoing stream of one-liners such as "good," "okay," "no," "wrong," etc., adds little to a student's feeling of well-being in the classroom. Feedback has proved to be a powerful tool in motivating students and ensuring the correctness of original learning (Hunter, 1986). Praise can and should be used to *extend pupil-teacher contact* and to encourage and reinforce desired behaviors. Yet, there is significant evidence to support the idea that less able students actually receive less praise than higher-achieving students (Good and Brophy, 1984). This was true even when less able students provided correct answers.

This pattern of inequality was evidenced in the teacher's willingness to accept student feelings (Adams and Biddle, 1970); listen to students (Rest, 1979); accept feelings (Brophy and Good, 1984); and show personal interest (Perkins, 1965).

Hunter (1985) has provided a vehicle to help ensure that students receive appropriate and intended feedback to their responses. She suggests that each student comment/response should be "dignified" so that the student feels he/she has made an important contribution to the class. Secondly, the teachers should "probe" for the correct answer so that the students in the class will receive appropriate information. Finally, regardless of correctness of student response, he/she should be held "accountable" for providing information relative to the topic at a future time during the lesson.

Thus, an incorrect student response should be followed by a clarifying statement emphasizing the correct and/or thoughtful parts of a student's comments; then, through a series of direct questions, the teacher should help "draw out" the correct response; and finally, regardless of the success achieved by the student, he/she is given credit for his/her contributions and told that he/she will be again asked to share his/her thoughts at a later time in the lesson.

Teachers must actively seek opportunities to provide personal contact and regard for the at-risk student. The concern and interest a teacher may have for the child, while in the classroom, may be the only opportunity throughout the child's entire day that sentiments about his/her self-worth can be developed. Thus, teachers should plan personal encounters with the at-risk child. Comments related to positive feelings about a child's school work, athletic or aesthetic skills, class, playground or cafeteria behavior, personal grooming, dress, etc., may provide the sense of security and worth needed to integrate the child into the mainstream of school life.

Effectively teaching and supporting the efforts of identified at-risk elementary students is a difficult task. Yet, it becomes critical that all educators continue to review the large body of knowledge embodied in effective schools and teacher effectiveness research to guide school and classroom practices. Moreover, they must go about this task with a high degree of *commitment and enthusiasm*. This enthusiasm in the classroom can manifest itself through the high energy level an individual teacher can generate as well as by the personal, genuine variable sincerity and encouragement a teacher shares with a child. Thus, concepts related to a teacher's inherent personality and/or "style" may have little to do with a child's perception of which teachers genuinely care about their profession, school, or most importantly, about students. Instead, it is more important that each teacher behaves in a manner that clearly sends a message of enthusiasm and support.

The "Classroom Wellness Inventory" (see Figure 2) can be used by teachers to assess the overall learning climate in their classrooms. Consistently high scores help ensure adherence to the concepts related to the positive student outcomes previously discussed. This inventory is not intended to provide categorical evidence as to the degree of wellness in a class. Thus, an overall optimum score is not provided. Instead, each item should be studied separately, with the assumption that improving a particular classroom phenomenon will ultimately improve the overall nature of classroom climate and student learning (Ogden and Germinario, 1988).

*Planning*

Planning for the establishment of climate and the effective use of class time are as important as planning for the delivery of content. All too often teachers spend a disproportionate amount of time planning for what to teach and not enough time considering how to teach. Studies of elementary school teachers have found that the amount of time the teacher actually uses for instruction may vary between 50 and 90 percent of the total school time available to them (Stallings, Hawley, Rosenholtz, et al.). All students, particularly at-risk students, benefit by the oppor-

Following is a list of descriptive statements which are associated with the promotion of learning in the classroom. Indicate the degree to which you think your classroom matches the description. There is no passing score. Areas in which you rate your classroom below 5 are areas in which improvement can be expected to result in increased learning.

|  | Low | | | | High |
|---|---|---|---|---|---|
| 1. The following groups of students have absentee rates of less than 5%: | | | | | |
|     a. High Achieving | 1 | 2 | 3 | 4 | 5 |
|     b. Average | 1 | 2 | 3 | 4 | 5 |
|     c. Low Achieving | 1 | 2 | 3 | 4 | 5 |
| 2. I am absent less than 3.5% of the time. | 1 | 2 | 3 | 4 | 5 |
| 3. I maximize classroom instruction time by: | | | | | |
|     a. Having clear standard procedures for classroom management | 1 | 2 | 3 | 4 | 5 |
|     b. Having materials and activities organized in advance | 1 | 2 | 3 | 4 | 5 |
| 4. Students in my class do not interrupt when I am speaking. | 1 | 2 | 3 | 4 | 5 |
| 5. Students in my class respect each other when they are asking or answering a question. | 1 | 2 | 3 | 4 | 5 |
| 6. Students are accepting of differences among their fellow students. | 1 | 2 | 3 | 4 | 5 |
| 7. I am aware when a student is having a personal problem and communicate my understanding. | 1 | 2 | 3 | 4 | 5 |
| 8. I do not think of the children who learn at a slower rate as a burden. | 1 | 2 | 3 | 4 | 5 |
| 9. I encourage gifted students to take intellectual risks and use higher level thinking skills. | 1 | 2 | 3 | 4 | 5 |
| 10. Students in my class feel successful. | 1 | 2 | 3 | 4 | 5 |
| 11. Each lesson I teach includes: | | | | | |
|     a. An objective communicated to the class | 1 | 2 | 3 | 4 | 5 |
|     b. Direct instruction of content | 1 | 2 | 3 | 4 | 5 |
|     c. Assessment of what was learned | 1 | 2 | 3 | 4 | 5 |
|     d. Summary activity | 1 | 2 | 3 | 4 | 5 |
| 12. Students work with other students of varying ability and in whole group activities. | 1 | 2 | 3 | 4 | 5 |
| 13. Students are not labeled by other students, by me, or by the way I organize the class. | 1 | 2 | 3 | 4 | 5 |
| 14. All types of students respond to an equal number of questions. | 1 | 2 | 3 | 4 | 5 |
| 15. I wait as long for answers from students of lesser ability as I do for those of higher ability. | 1 | 2 | 3 | 4 | 5 |
| 16. I assess the achievement of my students frequently and modify my instruction to meet needs. | 1 | 2 | 3 | 4 | 5 |
| 17. Students achieve the objectives of the curriculum and are ready for the next level class. | 1 | 2 | 3 | 4 | 5 |
| 18. I communicate with parents in a manner which has them support what is happening in class. | 1 | 2 | 3 | 4 | 5 |

*Figure 2. Maximizing Learning – Classroom Wellness Inventory.*

tunity and time needed for success. Wasting valuable time or engaging students in unimportant activities tends to lead to feelings of frustration and alienation that often manifest themselves in student misbehavior.

Teachers need to teach routines and clearly establish student expectations during the first few weeks of school. These procedures should become formalized and communicated to both students and parents. Effective teachers regulate learning activities. Common practices include sequencing course content so knowledge builds on itself, pacing instruction so students are prepared for the next step, monitoring success rates so all students stay productively engaged regardless of how quickly they learn, and running an orderly, academically focused classroom that keeps wasted time and misbehavior to a minimum. The establishment and reinforcement of routines will enhance student time-on-task, provide avenues for student success, develop feelings of classroom security and predictability, and increase opportunities for parents to ensure that their child is meeting classroom responsibilities.

### Instructional Management

The establishment of classroom routines provides a framework for the successful delivery of content and the systematic strategies aimed at promoting success for the at-risk student. This emphasis on the effective use of class time and teaching sequence can provide reliable, planned opportunities for student success.

Typically, effective instructional management begins with a diagnosis of students' prerequisite skills for the learning task. Subsequent instructions are broken down into small incremental steps or clusters from which learning gains have been reported (Brophy, 1981).

A preinstructional set is then established, which typically includes a clear statement of objective and expectation, a description of materials and procedures to be used, and an explanation of the significance of the task so that the lesson becomes more meaningful to students. Further, establishing this mental set is used to:

- build interest and develop willingness
- provide advance organization on a common frame of reference for lesson to follow
- relate clearly what is to follow
- provide a logical ''jumping off'' point for the lesson (Bruce, 1976)

The teacher must then provide specific instruction directed toward the achievement of lesson objectives. This active instruction from the teacher has been proven to show measurable learning dividends (Brophy and Good, 1985). Such active instruction should include mechanisms to actively involve students in learning. Provisions must be made for the ongoing monitoring of student understanding, demonstrations and other opportunities for learning through observation and imitation (modeling). Finally, sufficient time must be allocated for students to practice a new skill under the direct supervision of the teacher. During this practice time, the teacher walks among the students providing support, encouragement, praise, individual assistance, etc. Through this monitoring of student performance, a teacher is given an opportunity to use a number of behaviors that have proven to be directly related to achievement and student well being.

A specific time must be given at the end of the learning activity to summarize learning outcomes and to provide the opportunity for students to demonstrate understanding of the skills/concepts taught. This activity is crucial in ensuring that students have satisfactorily learned and practiced the correct skill. If not sufficiently checked, students may simply practice and reinforce errors. Although some students may quickly correct their mistakes, enough evidence exists that at-risk students are more likely to feel alienated from the task when making mistakes and experience a sense of hopelessness concerning their ability to succeed.

## Pupil Control

Effective teachers have the ability to minimize potential classroom problems by anticipating them and planning proactive responses to minor disciplinary disturbances They realize that when minor misbehavior is not eliminated immediately, there is an increased risk of an escalation of the misbehavior, increased loss of task time and the need for direct (and often negative) teacher intervention. Cummings (1983) provides an approach to dealing with minor classroom disturbances that fills the gap between simply ignoring the students' inappropriate behavior and forceful, negative intervention. The approach organizes teacher response on a continuum using behaviors that take little time and little interruption to the learning environment (i.e., eye contact, physical closeness, etc.).

The goals of this continuum of choices are:

- to maintain a positive feeling tone in the classroom
- to maximize time-on-task
- to present the teacher as a positive role model
- to avoid students' generalized negative feelings toward teacher, school, and subject

(For a complete list of minimal intervention strategies, see Cummings, *Managing to Teach*, 1983.)

## SUMMARY

The purpose of this chapter was to provide a basis for the identification of at-risk elementary students. Additionally, special care was given to sensitize school personnel to the importance of academic achievement and school success as the primary vehicles to prevent dysfunctional student behavior.

The understanding of the concepts and the systematic application of the teaching strategies discussed in this chapter will lead to higher levels of achievement for all elementary students and help provide a foundation of success for those students identified as being at high risk for school failure.

# CHAPTER 3

# Promoting Student Well-Being— The Role of the Elementary Principal

A CONSISTENT BODY of research points to the principal's role in establishing and maintaining a climate conducive to student learning and well-being. Perceptions of school climate tend to have a significant impact on the functioning of students and staff. Evidence exists that the learning environment or climate is a critical element that can be either conducive or detrimental to student success. Thus, the successful manipulation of the environmental, attitudinal, and programmatic variables available to an elementary school principal will prompt changes in student learning and school behavior.

"Unfriendly schools" tend to promote student disengagement by establishing real or perceived obstacles to student success. These obstacles lead to feelings of isolation, alienation, and ultimately, feelings of failure. It is the principal's expressed responsibility to promote programmatic, organizational, operational, and attitudinal initiatives, ensuring a healthy school climate that fosters student well-being and actively seeks ways to provide successful intervention for the at-risk student.

This chapter will identify and describe curricular and programmatic initiatives that help reduce elementary students' risk of failure. Additionally, the chapter will explore commonly used strategies that have proven to be ineffective for addressing the needs of the young at-risk student, as well as those that have proven to work. Finally, an operational design for the organization of a team approach for identifying and managing student risk will be described.

## CREATING A PRODUCTIVE SCHOOL CLIMATE

While the individual teacher controls the climate within the classroom, the principal has the major responsibility of establishing school guides and norms. There is a consistent relationship between school environments and students' feelings and behavior in them (Strother, 1983). Principals must work diligently to ensure a positive school climate by establishing norms that are specifically aimed at fostering student success for all and strategies that help reclaim at-risk children. These efforts should be guided by activities that foster:

- a spirit of achievement that encourages teachers to set high expectations for themselves and their students
- a spirit of belonging that actively seeks to integrate students into the mainstream of school life
- a spirit of mastery that embraces the need for students to feel competent and in control of their learning outcomes
- a spirit of caring that increases the student's sense of self-worth by becoming committed to the positive value of helping others
- a spirit of cooperation that does not allow students to criticize themselves or allow others to criticize them
- a spirit of interdependence that accepts the need for student, parent, teacher, and principal collaboration in shaping a positive school climate

An effective educational program for elementary students does not require a change in the entire educational system; it does, however, take the vision of a committed professional to examine the environment that has been created for its students. It takes the dedicated leadership of the building principal to analyze current school practices in terms of their impact on student learning and well-being. Moreover, it takes courage and sustained effort on the part of the entire school community to modify existing school norms and teaching strategies to help ensure the effective programming for its at-risk students.

## CURRICULUM TO REDUCE RISK—WHAT DOESN'T WORK

### Retention

Requiring students to repeat a grade when they have not met minimal levels of academic competencies is a relatively common practice in schools. Many urban schools routinely hold back 15 or 20 percent of students at each grade level, and by grade ten, up to 60 percent of students in these schools have been retained at least once (Gottfredson, 1988).

Yet, as one of the most frequently used strategies to deal with at-risk students, it has proven to be the least effective (Slavin and Madden, 1989). Clearly, as a generic strategy to improve the learning potential for at-risk students, retention has not shown any consistent benefits over the length of a retained student's school career, as compared to students of similar age who were not held back (Shepard and Smith, 1989), and are at greater risk of dropping out of school (Natriello et al., 1990). Moreover, student retention tends to heighten a child's feeling of failure and, in many cases, create distress and shame for those students who fall behind.

Although the overall utility of retaining at-risk students is exceedingly questionable, there are rare times when retention may be beneficial. For example, very young children may not be so sensitive to being held back and may benefit from the additional time to compensate for development lags or significant skill deficiencies. Similarly, the decision to retain a student at a transitional point, such as from elementary to middle school, may help break a pattern of academic failure if the child and his/her parents are supportive of the retention.

If individual decisions for student retention are pursued, it is important to establish a framework for success in the repeated grade. Further, the student's program must not be simply a repeat of the previous year's school program. An individualized approach, capitalizing on the retained student's established skill base, his/her unique learning style and his/her need for social integration must be promoted. In most cases, these needs prompt a change in the established grade curriculum, the teacher and, at times, the school.

### Tracking and Ability Grouping

A common practice thought to be an effective strategy in dealing with student academic diversity is to separate children into different learning classes or groups based on a teacher's perception of a student's readiness to learn or on a student's previous academic achievement. Generally referred to as tracking, this practice in some form is almost universal in American secondary schools, and is increasingly prominent in the nation's middle and elementary schools (Braddock, 1990).

At the elementary level, tracking most often occurs by subgrouping students within otherwise heterogeneous classrooms. In theory, these groups are formulated to better serve the diverse academic needs and interests of students. The research on the outcomes of this practice, however, demonstrates a wide variety of negative effects on those students placed in "lower achieving" tracks (Office of Educational Research and Improvement, U.S. Department of Education, 1990).

Specifically, in a thorough review of both the intent and actual effects of tracking, Jeannie Oakes (1985) acknowledges that tracking is a well-intended practice based on the seemingly logical assumption that a teacher teaches more effectively when students are grouped homogeneously by ability levels. Yet, in reality, students placed in lower tracks receive a poorer-quality education than students in higher tracks. She concludes that this effect can be measured in terms of student achievement, school relationships with peers, student self-concept and motivation, and vocational education.

There are a number of variables that lead to this negative effect. Typically, students in lower tracks are offered a less challenging curriculum, the instructional pace is slower, fewer demands are made in learning higher-order skills, and test and homework assignments are taken less seriously (Mitchell, 1990).

Thus, tracking as a school or classroom response to meeting the needs of low-achieving, at-risk elementary students actually functions in ways that are detrimental to these students' achievement levels and feelings of self-worth. Wheelock and Dorman (1988) conclude that it is not surprising that the at-risk students assess the status of their school placement and suspect that the decision to place them in such tracks have judged them "losers."

### Pullout Programs

Removing elementary students from their regularly scheduled classroom for remedial instruction is a common practice in our nation's schools (Berman et al., 1987). Yet, at best, these programs may only keep students from falling behind their classmates (Carter, 1984).

Although organizationally convenient, instructional delivery strategy pullout programs tend to promote labelling of students and may add to a student's feeling of isolation and alienation. Additionally, instruction in pullout programs often lacks integration with regular classroom instruction, causing the at-risk student to fall further behind the mainstream activities of his/her class.

Caution should be used when organizing a "pullout program" for dealing with the at-risk behaviors of elementary students. Schools may wish to use pullouts to deal with isolated problems on a short-term basis.

Promoting pullout programs as the basis for addressing the needs of at-risk students is exceedingly suspect (Slavin and Madden, 1989).

### Unnecessary Labelling

With the adoption of Public Law 94-142, every state and local school district was compelled to provide free, appropriate education for all handicapped children. As a result of this law, children previously excluded or neglected by schools are now included and benefitting.

Along with this progress have come some predictable difficulties. The most profound has been the vast increase in the number of students who are seemingly in need of specialized services. Studies of learning disabled students reveal that they are usually the lowest of the low achievers, with no other distinctive characteristics (Deshler et al., 1982). As a dramatic one-time response to low achievement, in elementary schools these students are typically placed in ''pullout'' programs, which may act as a detriment to successful education.

Often the specialized placement causes a certain stigmatization that segregates the special education students from their peers and their regular school activities. Frequently, the results are lowered academic and social expectations on the part of the students themselves, as well as their peers and their teachers (Will, 1986). Thus, in many cases, students who may not be developmentally ready to address a learning objective or who (for whatever reason) are reluctant to get involved in learning activities may receive specialized placement simply because no other avenues of prevention have been established.

It is not the author's intent to minimize the need for specialized services for handicapped children. Yet, school leaders must look carefully at instructional vehicles routinely used for the mildly handicapped or otherwise educationally at-risk students before prompting special education alternatives.

## PRACTICES THAT ACCELERATE THE IMPACT OF SCHOOL FAILURE

All too often, at-risk students are likely to interpret common school rules and practices as a signal that they must either conform or leave. Many times the uniqueness of the at-risk youngsters makes it quite difficult for them to either understand or relate to traditional institutionalized school norms. It is not the author's intent to establish distinct standards of acceptable behavior for at-risk students. Yet, enough common sense and empirical evidence exists to support the need for schools to examine the impact of standard rules and patterns of punishment on its most vulnerable students.

### School Attendance Policies

Many at-risk elementary students respond to their feelings of alienation and failure by simply not attending school. Imaginary illnesses, purposeful oversleeping, and at times "cutting" school are not uncommon methods for these students to avoid their negative feelings about school. Further, these problems are compounded when parents are either ill-equipped or negligent in their ability to get their children to school.

Obviously, a high rate of student absence is both a cause and effect of increased alienation and often can predict, with a high degree of certainty, if an elementary student will eventually drop out of school (Kaeser, 1985).

Often student attendance problems are met with punitive, impersonal, exclusionary, or ambivalent school responses that create more feelings of hostility and rejection. Unfortunately, school attendance policies typically do little to address core problems such as conflicts with teachers or peers, family dysfunction, or repeated academic defeats that often underlie student absences (Wheelock and Dorman, 1988).

Schools must develop and communicate procedures that focus on the message that the school values attendance and will provide the necessary support to assist parents to foster regular school attendance for their children. Additionally, appropriate follow-up on absences, particularly through personal contact, should be undertaken in ways that show concern rather than condemnation. Finally, incentives for good attendance and opportunities for making up work should be developed to further encourage student attendance and success.

### School Discipline and Suspension

Many elementary students who are at risk for school failure come to school with significant family dysfunction, or they misbehave in response to their frustration with their school or life experiences. Paradoxically, disruptive behavior is both a symptom of a student's underlying alienation from school and a cause for ongoing rejection from the institution (Welhage and Rutter, 1986).

At-risk students appear to be particularly receptive to personal as opposed to institutional authority (Natriello, 1987). Young children in particular must be counselled as to the nature of school rules; also, they must clearly understand the cause and effect relationships of their actions. Often this personalized approach through a counselor or mentor is more effective than a general application of school rules.

Addressing disruptive behavior by the use of out-of-school suspensions often reinforces the at-risk student's feelings of not belonging, and clearly adds to the negative effects of poor school attendance. If at all possible, schools should utilize structured, supervised, in-school suspension as a response to continued student misbehavior. This setting can provide a vehicle for keeping a student in school, where he/she can learn and receive the necessary academic and emotional support to help avoid recurring disciplinary problems.

Most importantly, elementary students must be taught the difference between punishment and discipline. They must be taught methods of avoiding situations that lead to disciplinary problems and techniques to negotiate conflicts or talk about their feelings *before they engage in disruptive behaviors*.

## *Conclusion*

School administrators need to examine current school practice as it relates to the negative impact of the common practices outlined above. This examination should lead schools to choices regarding their responses to the failure of their students. Ultimately, those practices that continue to have no or negative consequences on the at-risk student should be discontinued.

The remainder of this chapter will be devoted to those school practices that do work, effectively programming an elementary school's at-risk population for academic success.

## CURRICULUM TO REDUCE RISK—WHAT DOES WORK

### *Preschool Experience*

Early enrichment and preacademic preparation can be a significant factor in providing a framework for success for the at-risk youngster. These programs should emphasize language development, preliteracy skills, and activities that foster self-esteem.

Although research tends to find strong effects in the language and I.Q. scores of disadvantaged children immediately after the preschool experience, these effects tend to diminish each subsequent year until, by the second or third grade, they are relatively undetectable (Karweit, 1989). Thus, as an isolated strategy, preschool is not likely to substantially reduce the risk of school failure in and of itself; it can, however, get students off to a good start in their educational experience.

Preschool enrichment must also begin in the home by providing parents with the knowledge and resources to help their children. Reviewing school records to identify families with high-risk, school-age children can serve as a starting point for identifying and involving parents in preschool programs. Similarly, the importance of increasing the learning opportunities in the homes of at-risk youngsters must not be overlooked as a major preschool learning strategy.

In summary, for disadvantaged children in particular, preschool programs offered in conjunction with parent education, meals, and other health and social services, can provide a sound foundation for early school success (Phlegar, 1987).

### First Grade Prevention Programs

Several effective instructional programs are built on the proposition that success in first grade, particularly in reading, is a prerequisite for success later in school (Slavin, 1989). Of all the first grade prevention programs Slavin examined, those programs that used tutoring and/or small group instruction were extremely successful in increasing students' reading achievement. Reading recovery systems, whereby students are tutored by specially trained teachers for thirty minutes a day for at least sixty days, was the only prevention program that showed long-term positive effects in student reading achievement (DeFord et al., 1987). In a similar study, dealing exclusively with first graders, Boehnlein (1987) found that students at highest risk for failure receiving thirty to forty hours of daily, intensive one-on-one reading recovery lessons never needed any additional remediation to maintain their skill levels.

### Peer Tutoring

The power of peer and cross-age tutoring is frequently overlooked in spite of the fact that this strategy can produce as much as two times the achievement of computer-assisted instruction, three times the achievement of reducing class size from thirty-five to thirty students, and close to four times the results of lengthening the school day by one hour (Jenkins and Jenkins, 1987). In addition to improved academic gains, at-risk elementary students often benefit from the caring and role-modeling of a "big brother" or "big sister."

To be successful, tutorial programs must be guided by three elements: training of tutors, ongoing program management, and accurate record keeping and evaluation.

Effective training is a critical component to the success of such a strategy. Simply placing adolescents in tutorial situations without prior training can produce no effect and at times even negative effects on student learning. Peer tutors must be trained to understand the nature of their roles, effective communication and interpersonal skills, as well as specific tutorial teaching techniques.

Peer tutors must realize their role to be one of academic and, at times, social support. Clearly, they are not to act as counselors or advisors to a student who is being tutored. Despite the possible age differential between the students, the peer tutor is not mature enough to serve any role beyond the one prescribed within the tutorial teaching model.

The peer tutoring programs must also be managed on an ongoing basis. The professional staff members coordinating the program must share responsibility for recruiting, screening, selecting, and training the peer tutors. Additionally, careful plans should be made to provide periodic meetings with the tutors to reinforce their roles, extend training, and provide needed support.

Finally, it is exceedingly important that the peer tutors keep accurate records of the content, activities, and achievement levels related to the student receiving the tutoring. In summary, peer tutoring is an easily initiated, cost-effective way to extend the learning experience for the at-risk student. Equally important, by harnessing the power of positive peer pressure, the young at-risk student can link more closely with benefits of school achievement and adolescent success.

### Mentoring

Providing a personal, ongoing support system is critical to the success of at-risk elementary students. Often these students do not have adequate role models or nurturing home environments to enrich their lives. Through the use of in-school *mentors*, identified at-risk students have the opportunity to get one-on-one academic assistance, counseling, personal attention, school advocacy, and the sense that someone in the school truly cares about what happens to them.

Mentoring is a relatively simple process by which a dedicated staff member volunteers to be paired with an identified at-risk student with whom he/she is to maintain frequent contact. The general goal of this program is to personalize the school experience for the child by providing ongoing support and advocacy for the child's success. In this role, the staff member who serves as a mentor may engage in the following activities:

- Act as a "cheerleader" for the child's efforts at school, at home, and in the community.
- Meet individually with the child to demonstrate a genuine, personal interest in the student's concerns and aspirations.
- Help in the organization and completion of school responsibilities and assignments.
- Maintain open lines of communication with the student's parents.

Mentor programs can be organized in a variety of different ways. Administrators, teachers, and custodial or other support staff can be trained to be effective mentors. Additionally, community members can be used as student mentors. In some school districts, senior citizens have been utilized as mentors; the wealth of life experiences and the skills developed through effective parenting can easily be transferred to the mentoring setting. The use of senior citizens can be exceedingly effective with primary grade students who often view the mentor as a grandparent. "Grandma" or "grandpa" may provide the necessary love and support often missing in the lives of at-risk youngsters.

Again, it is important that those who serve as mentors understand their respective roles and responsibilities. These volunteers are not trained in nor should they attempt in-depth counseling. Instead, their training should reinforce their roles as tutors, advocates, and friends for the young at-risk students. Additionally, they should be trained to identify serious problems such as child abuse, thoughts of suicide, and drug abuse so that they can route the appropriate referral to those school professionals or social welfare agencies who are more specifically trained in these very complex situations.

Despite the variety of approaches a mentor program can take, it has proven to be a viable strategy to enrich the learning and life potential for at-risk youngsters. In a recent study conducted by the American Federation of Teachers, mentor programs have proven to play a significant role in helping students to be more successful in school (Glass, 1991). However, it is important that these programs clearly understand the particular needs of their target groups and structure services in a way that meets those specific needs.

### Extended Weekends or Summer Tutorial Programs

Academic, social, and emotional gains that may have resulted from the initiation of strategies specifically aimed at helping the at-risk elementary student can often be lost if appropriate follow-up and monitoring are not continued outside the scope of the normal school day. It is important that schools look for ways to extend their influence on the identified at-risk student.

Using paid or volunteer professional staff members or community volunteers such as the local PTA, civic association members interested in service projects, or extending the mentorship concept are just a few of the ways that weekend and/or summer tutorial programs can be promoted. Once trained, any of these groups could easily provide a valuable extended support system for the at-risk youngster.

To be successful, school personnel need to coordinate and monitor the program. Ideally, the program should take place within the school. However, if this is not possible, a local town hall or recreation center, church hall, etc., would easily serve as a central meeting place for the tutors and students. Special care should be given to providing directed instruction aimed at maintaining, reinforcing, or enriching identified skill areas. Additionally, these skills should be closely linked to the sequential school curriculum so that students can easily integrate their learnings into the existing school curriculum.

### Cooperative Learning

An increasing amount of research points to a wide variety of positive academic and affective outcomes associated with cooperative learning. Although a number of models exist, they all generally include students working in small teams engaging in learning activities aimed at mastering material initially presented by the teacher.

All cooperative learning methods require students to perform highly structured group tasks. These tasks emphasize group goals while maintaining individual accountability. Despite the difference among cooperative learning methods, they share these general characteristics:

- Classes are divided into small groups with two to six members.
- Clearly defined objectives are specified for the groups.
- A cooperative environment and a reward system are present.
- Students support each other's efforts to achieve.
- Group member behavior is monitored (Educational Research Service, 1990).

Although not a panacea for all the needs of students, the use of cooperative learning strategies has resulted in improvements both in the achievement of students and in the quality of their interpersonal relations. In "Synthesis of Research on Cooperative Learning," Slavin (1991) found a wide range of benefits associated with cooperative learning strategies:

- Of sixty-seven high-quality studies that measured the effects of cooperative learning on achievement, 61 percent found significantly greater achievement in cooperative classrooms than in control classes.
- In those studies where variations on cooperative learning included the two essential elements of *group goals* and *individual accountability*, 84 percent of the studies showed significantly more positive achievement for cooperative learning students.
- Effects on achievement have been consistent for students at different ability levels and for students of different ethnic groups.
- Numerous studies have shown that cooperative learning has a positive impact on the acceptance of handicapped mainstreamed students by other students.
- Some studies have shown that cooperative learning has a positive effect on the self-esteem of students.
- Some studies have also shown that cooperative learning has a positive impact on how much students like school, the development of peer norms in favor of doing well academically, feelings of student control over their destinies, cooperativeness, altruism, and student time-on-task.

(For a comprehensive review of cooperative learning concepts and strategies, see Johnson et al., *Circles of Learning*, 1986, and Slavin, *Cooperative Learning*, 1983.)

## Computer-Assisted Instruction

At-risk learners frequently do not respond to the traditional approaches presented within the classroom. Alternative instructional strategies that capitalize on the elementary at-risk student's unique learning style and emotional needs may be needed to foster motivation and success. The use of computers can be helpful in providing such an alternative.

Computers can control the amount, sequence, and at times the mastery of skills. This can be accomplished at a pace consistent with the student's ability while providing instant feedback and reinforcement. Additionally, by using this individualized approach, at-risk students are saved from the embarrassment of making errors or moving at a pace slower than the rest of the class. Although not promoted as the only instructional strategy to be used, the use of computers may provide a motivational incentive for reluctant learners.

One particular application of computers for elementary-age students that has proven successful has been developed by Stanley Pogrow. The Higher-Order Thinking Skills (HOTS) program, while appropriate for all elementary students, was initially developed to deal with particular learning problems of remedial students. The objective of the program is to help at-risk elementary students master the basic thinking processes that underlie all learning.

The HOTS program is being used with remedial at-risk youngsters throughout the country. In many cases, this program has successfully improved student basic skills achievement, enriched student problem-solving skills, and appears to have a positive relationship to student self-confidence and language fluency (Pogrow, 1988).

## Parental Involvement

Increasingly, researchers are learning that parents have a crucial role to play in the education of their children and that the more contact there is between teachers and parents, the greater the gains of the students (Epstein, 1989). One reason for the impact of parent involvement tends to be related to student motivation. In most cases, parents appear to be the primary influences in a child's motivation to learn (Jaynes, 1990).

It is essential, then, that schools develop strategies to actively involve the parents of at-risk elementary students in their children's education. Very often parents are aware of the unacceptable behavior of their children; but they don't know how to address the problems. Often schools must take a rudimentary approach, providing parenting classes for parents. During these classes, concepts related to the development of active listening and communication skills, the setting of expectations, discipline in the home, child nutrition, and creation of the appropriate learning environment must be addressed. Additionally, parents must be made aware of both public and private agencies that can provide assistance to the child and/or family if the scope of the child's problem is beyond the scope of the school program.

Schools must develop a climate where parents feel comfortable in coming to the school. Tours during the school day can help parents understand the environment in which their children learn. "Welcome Wagons" composed of school personnel and parents can help integrate newcomers into the school community. Home visits by school personnel consistent with the parents' work schedule show that the school is genuinely concerned about the well-being of the child. These strategies are both cost-effective and easily implemented into the school's community relations program.

### Elementary Student Assistance Teams

A student assistance team provides the necessary focus to all activities aimed at identifying and intervening in the lives of at-risk students. Typically, the team is composed of the school principal, school nurse, a member of the district's special education team, and teachers. Each member is given distinct responsibilities related to the school's efforts to program for its at-risk population.

Although their roles may differ from school to school, essentially team members engage in similar activities such as:

- facilitating the accumulation of information regarding referred students
- meeting with teachers to determine the nature of risk
- working cooperatively with teachers and parents to develop an intervention plan for use in and out of school
- monitoring the relative success of the program
- acting as liaison to outside community agencies
- providing inservice instruction to staff and parents
- communicating the philosophy and goals of the program

The use of a team approach helps to increase recognition throughout the school for the need to intervene in the lives of at-risk youngsters. It also provides a systematic way to identify and program for the at-risk student (see Figure 1). It provides an ongoing collaborative support system for classroom teachers. Finally, it provides a mechanism to monitor the school's efforts to help its most needy clients.

Because of the significance of this strategy, a complete review of student assistance team's goals, procedures and ongoing strategies will be presented in subsequent chapters.

## SUMMARY

This chapter described the role of the elementary principal in the development of a school program aimed at identifying and remediating at-risk youngsters. Common elementary school practices that tended respectively to inhibit and promote success for the elementary at-risk student were explored.

Through the understanding of the use of the curricular strategies discussed in this chapter, it is hoped that the elementary principal can effectively assume the necessary leadership role in the prevention of and programming for at-risk students.

# CHAPTER 4

# Promoting Student Well-Being — The Role of Central Administration and School Board

IT IS REASONABLE to assume that every school district would be eager to establish immediate programs to meet the needs of its at-risk population; yet, isolated program initiatives may only serve to diffuse the school's overall effort to educate its students. Instead, schools should look toward a sustained effort in most aspects of school programs and operations. A prevention/intervention disposition must become part of the school's vision, with efforts aimed at meeting the needs of its at-risk population as systematically planned as one would plan a math or reading program.

## CREATING A COMMITMENT FOR PROGRAM DEVELOPMENT

If programs aimed at educating at-risk populations are to be effective, they must become a priority for the entire organization and goals, policies, and strategies for conceptual and financial support must be carefully developed. The first step in this process is to educate the local school board and community as to the need for prevention and intervention strategies in its elementary schools. The responsibility primarily belongs to the superintendent and his/her immediate administrative staff.

The school community must be convinced that there are children in its elementary schools who run a serious risk of school and life failure, and that the school has an expressed responsibility to develop strategies to address this ever-increasing phenomenon in our schools. Unfortunately, many times the school community and its representatives on school boards (particularly in nonurban districts) fail to recognize the existence of school problems related to the at-risk youngster. Similarly, if convinced that a problem may exist, they may often conclude that the origins and nature of the problem exist outside of the school, thus abdicating any school responsibility beyond that of the formal, content curriculum.

The school community must constantly be made aware of its responsibility to program for the success of all students. Additionally, school boards, as with the school's staff, must become committed to the development and ongoing support for programs that foster an inviting school climate for all students and more specifically for, initiatives that direct resources toward its most needy students.


### Policy Development

The degree to which programs and policies reflect the level of support for at-risk initiatives depends on the particular character of the student population served. Some schools may need only modest plans, while others may effectively become intensive care units (New Jersey School Board Association, 1990). Thus, the logical starting point in the implementation of a successful program is to assess the nature of risk in the district's elementary school age population. Through a comprehensive needs assessment, representatives of the entire school community can provide the conceptual framework that should guide at-risk programming.

It is important that a district-wide steering committee be formed to initiate this process. This committee should be led by the school superintendent. This is an important element since genuine concern and commitment must be established at the top of the educational hierarchy. Additionally, members of the school board, teaching staff, school support staff, local government and police, county or regional youth services officials, parent-teacher associations, civic associations, clergy, and other interested ''communities'' must be represented on this committee.

The primary function of this committee is to collect and analyze data so that the school community can better understand the character of the district's student body. Additionally, through both a formal and informal assessment, the leadership of the committee must be able to present its findings to the school board and the community at large so that the need for program support is established and the parameters for program planning are developed. It is at this point that a *mission statement* for the at-risk program is presented and integrated into the generic district goals.

This mission statement should be presented in a direct manner and easily incorporated into existing district goals. For example, recognition and commitment for at-risk programming can be added to long-standing goals for the district's guidance and counseling efforts:

> To provide quality services for all students in the areas of academic and career planning, guidance and counseling *while insuring that measures are taken to identify and assist students at-risk*. (Moorestown Public School District, 1990, Moorestown, New Jersey, amended district goals)

### Planning for Program Success

Following formal school board adoption of the mission statement, the steering committee's next major responsibility is to organize planning committees in areas related to program development, utilization and training of staff, and the development of networks for ongoing involvement and support.

These planning committees activities should be focused around four central themes:

(*1*) What is the status of school programs in relationship to the mission statement?

(*2*) What programs or activities exist that should be incorporated into the school's at-risk program?

(*3*) What resources does the school need to promote selected program strategies?

(*4*) What does the school specifically have to do to implement its strategies?

Discussions surrounding each of these questions should result in specific strategies, responsibilities, and standards for assessing program effectiveness. Moreover, planning outcomes must be operationalized in terms of curriculum plans, facilities, staffing, materials, lesson plans, in-service training, and budget (see Chapter 18 for a sample three-year set of process and outcome objectives for student assistance).

This framework for systematized program development is closely linked to the *strategic planning process*. This process provides a rationale framework for planning while establishing a mechanism for broad-based staff and community involvement in program decisions. (For a complete review of strategic planning in an educational organization, see McCune, *Guide for Strategic Planning for Educators*, 1986.)

## PROGRAM DEVELOPMENT

The at-risk program in the elementary schools must be developed around three major components: *prevention, intervention, and aftercare* (see Figure 3).

Prevention activities, many of which have been discussed in previous chapters, must provide an organizational and curricular format by which the school can actively promote student learning and well-being. This begins by an examination of current school organization and practices that impact on student learning and self-esteem. This also includes the development of school curriculum that addresses topics related to life and to drug resistance skills, such as *Here's Looking at You, 2000* (Roberts et al., 1986). Additionally, teacher training in those instructional strategies must be closely linked to student achievement and well-being. Finally, student assistance teams must be developed to foster a prevention mentality throughout the school and to support teachers and parents of identified at-risk students.

Intervention should include all planned and spontaneous responses to the identified at-risk student. Clearly, these strategies should be carefully matched with the identified needs of the targeted students. Yet, general actions that can be initiated in elementary schools include, but are not limited to:

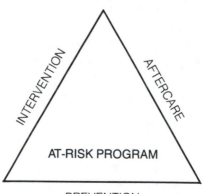

*Figure 3. At-Risk Program Components.*

- modifying the student's program so that the child meets with more academic and/or personal success
- providing more group activities, such as in-common reading, so that students in the low reading groups work regularly with the total class, allowing the opportunity to interact with positive peer models
- changing the physical arrangement of the class so that certain students can be separated or encouraged to work together
- avoiding classroom activities that emphasize competition, which may lead to consistent feelings of failure
- providing an ongoing system for teachers to explore problem-solving techniques
- providing individual counseling with principals
- using cooperative learning groups in the classroom
- employing behavior modification strategies
- instituting a peer tutoring/buddy system
- assigning an instructional aide to the student
- making available in-house support services (physical education, reading specialist, nurse, art, music, speech, and language) to the student on a short-term basis
- offering mentorships
- ensuring referral to a special education team for consultation or comprehensive evaluation
- referring to outside agencies
- referring to volunteer student assistance support services, e.g., grandparents, psychological counseling, and Adopt-a-School
- maintaining contact with home (daily or weekly monitoring)
- ensuring referral to Basic Skills Improvement Program
- providing group and/or individual support services if deemed applicable by the primary prevention counselor

(The above list is adapted from *The Elementary Student Assistance Resource Handbook*, with the permission of the Moorestown Public Schools, Moorestown, New Jersey.)

No at-risk program in the elementary schools can be considered comprehensive without an aftercare program. This component of the program is implemented when a child returns to school following a lengthy school absence caused by a life or family crisis. In many respects, aftercare is both a preventive and an intervention strategy directed at this targeted population. The main objective of aftercare activities is to provide a bridge for successful integration back into school following an extended absence. If the absence is caused by a life or family crisis such as death of a parent or sibling, recent parental separation or divorce, or extended serious illness, aftercare activities can provide the necessary counseling and support needed to refocus a child's attention to school and learning.

If the absence is caused by extended school suspension for disruptive behavior, aftercare activities can help the child better understand the cause and effect relationships for his/her behavior. Additionally, aftercare activities can provide a prescription for success so that the likelihood of recurring dysfunctional behavior is decreased. Finally, under any circumstance, the aftercare program provides opportunities for the school staff and parents to work collaboratively toward student problem resolution.

On occasion, particularly in the middle school years, children are confronted with and often are tempted toward experimental drug and alcohol use. The school's aftercare program is of significant value when a child is found to be abusing drugs or alcohol or when he/she returns from a substance abuse related school suspension. In this case, the aftercare program embodies specific objectives and processes.

The objectives of this program are to:

- educate students about chemical use
- educate students as to the identification of use, misuse, and addiction
- educate students as to the short- and long-term consequences of substance abuse
- educate students as to the impact of substance abuse on families
- build rapport between the student and the student assistance team in an attempt to encourage positive change in student behavior
- provide support for the student as he/she returns to school

The structure of the aftercare program is:

- a meeting between the parents, student, and student assistance team
- three educational/evaluation sessions for the student
- a review of the student's school performance by the student assistance team
- written notification to the parents and school administration that the student has completed aftercare; if necessary, suggestions

for future assistance are also provided at that time and a second parental meeting may be required

(This list is adapted from *The Middle School At-Risk Team Support (STARTS) Team Handbook*, with permission of the Moorestown Public Schools, Moorestown, New Jersey.)

## UTILIZATION AND TRAINING OF STAFF

Critical to the success of the at-risk program is a commitment by the school board and school administration to the training of staff in strategies related to the at-risk youngster. Obviously, the school staff must have a meaningful role in the development of the program. Yet, beyond an understanding of the program, staff training should be directed at generating interest, commitment, and support for instructional activities and program initiatives aimed at educating a school's at-risk population.

Specifically, topics that should be addressed include, but are not limited to:

- the nature of risk in elementary school students
- behavioral characteristics of the at-risk learner
- the impact of teacher expectations on student achievement
- strategies for the development of differential learning activities
- development of a positive class climate
- societal problems that influence child and adolescent development
- development of better understanding of dysfunctional student behavior, e.g., chronic academic failure, chronic disruptive behavior, drug abuse, bullying, potential suicide, or reaction to physical abuse
- understanding the role of school personnel with the at-risk program
- understanding and supporting the school's student assistance team
- effectively involving the parents of at-risk students

In addition to the valuable information and techniques the school staff can obtain from such training, involving staff in the ongoing evolution of the school's at-risk program gives them a sense of ownership in its success. As importantly, it guarantees input from the professionals who are closest to students and have the best understanding of how proposed solutions would work on an everyday basis (Brodinsky and Keough, 1989).

## NETWORK FOR ONGOING INVOLVEMENT AND SUPPORT

Public awareness and support are essential elements for successful prevention activities. Because the problems associated with at-risk students are so complex, boards of education should take full advantage of opportunities for community support. Through community awareness initiatives in school newsletters, school events, PTA events, and local media, public awareness concerning the complexities of life for school-age children and the need for public support of the school's efforts in this critical area can be promoted.

This public awareness and support may also assist the school in obtaining volunteers, mentors and, at times, financial support for the at-risk program. As with many school-sponsored programs, specific fundraising events can be sponsored with funds earmarked for a wide variety of prevention and intervention activities.

School officials should also become increasingly aware of the need to utilize those public and private organizations in their geographic areas that may help the quality of life for the at-risk youngster and his/her family. Cooperative relationships with organizations such as health and social service agencies, day care centers, recreation programs and churches are just a few resources that can actively assist the school and family with prevention and intervention activities (see Appendix A for additional resource agencies).

Districts should seriously consider developing linkages with local and broader-based businesses. As a community service, businesses often provide funds, professional expertise, equipment, and volunteers to help the school's efforts. For their part, schools should provide appropriate recognition of business involvement and contributions through publicity and awards (National School Board Association, 1989).

Finally, there is a wealth of opportunity for meaningful support through local, national, and international service clubs. Often Rotary, Lions, Kiwanis, and other such highly recognizable organizations are anxious to assist local schools through volunteers and financial support. Adopt-a-school type programs are frequently supported by such organizations. Additionally, these service organizations, primarily made up of successful men and women, can be a viable source of positive role models for at-risk elementary students.

## SUMMARY

A commitment toward programming for the success of at-risk elementary students is built on two essential principles: *prevention* and immediate *focused intervention*.

In previous chapters, a wide variety of strategies aimed at sensitizing school personnel to develop a "prevention mentality" were explored and developed.

This chapter dealt with the responsibilities of the district's Central Administration and School Board in the development of policies aimed at legitimizing the role of the school in remediating the needs of the at-risk elementary student. Additionally, strong emphasis was placed on the need for a systematic planning model to ensure the success and acceptance of the elementary school's at-risk program.

The next four chapters will address unique dysfunctions associated with elementary and middle school students. Specific strategies aimed at eliminating identified risks are explored in detail.

# PART TWO

# THE AT-RISK PROGRAM: DESIGN AND OPERATION

**IN THE PREVIOUS** chapters, guidelines were given for teachers, principals, central administrators, and school board members to establish and reinforce positive behaviors and supportive school climates. Although these efforts may include such preventative measures as the inclusion of social-emotional issues in both curriculum and teacher/parent training, many children will continue to experience difficulty in the elementary school setting. Educators must consider the needs of these students, as well as provide for the potential dysfunction of others. A formal mechanism should be established for the identification of and intervention in student problems. This mechanism should also provide for the involvement of parents in this process and for the monitoring and reassessment of intervention strategies. In many districts, the design and implementation of a student assistance program can provide these kinds of services in ways that involve all the resources of the school. In the chapters to follow, a blueprint for the design of such a program will be provided. Consideration will be given to tailoring these designs to the particular needs and existing resources of any school setting.

# CHAPTER 5

# *Program Design*

## GOALS OF THE PROGRAM

THE MISSION OF the school is learning. The goal of the student assistance program is to identify behaviors that are impeding the learning of students and to provide needed help so they can become productive learners and members of the school community.

Student assistance programs at the elementary level may be designed not only to assist the at-risk student, but to provide primary prevention activities to avert future difficulties for younger students. Many children enter school with serious disadvantages, lacking the necessary life skills and parental support to help them through their difficulties. Others experience a life trauma (death or divorce of a parent, catastrophic illness), lags in skill development, or temporary disadvantages such as limited English or other remedial needs. Although educators cannot control many of the variables and outside influences that interfere with children's ability to learn, provisions can be made for both planned and reactive attempts to assist.

Expectations for a program of this sort are often unrealistic. The program is not meant to provide treatment, nor to solve every problem and avert every crisis. Student assistance programs are not meant to supplant the other services of the school but to interweave them for the most complete and global assessments and interventions for children.

Finally, any proposed student assistance program requires the sanction of the board of education and the full support of the administration. Policies that encompass administrative code must provide the basis of the philosophy and procedures of the program (see Chapter 4).

## ENLISTING THE SUPPORT OF THE PROFESSIONAL STAFF

It is vital for all staff to understand the purposes of their student assistance program and, ideally, to accept it as an effective mechanism for helping children. Elegant flow charts that provide procedures and responses for all eventualities mean nothing without the sanction and support of the professional staff.

Before such a program is set forth, staff should have a decided role in defining the needs of the students previously unaddressed by the school. By involving the staff in acknowledging the need for an integrated response to these problems, the process of a shared vision can begin. Grade-level meetings that discuss specific areas of need, related to developmental stages as well as high-risk situations, can be invaluable in designing a program specifically tailored for a particular population.

## USE OF EXISTING RESOURCES

It is a common misconception that a school district cannot offer a student assistance program without counseling personnel. Naturally, the ideal situation would include counselors and clinicians, but the reality of many school districts is that elementary counseling personnel are considered frills. Even the mandated services of a special education child study team may be limited in the small proportion of time they can lend to the general education population.

How then can an elementary school, usually devoid of full-time counseling personnel, structure an effective program to identify, refer, and intervene with students? The following sections deal with suggestions for administrators to design a program that can offer varied and effective in-house interventions.

## THE STUDENT ASSISTANCE TEAM

Sometimes called the core team, this interdisciplinary group of staff members representing various roles and knowledge bases, can be an elegant, efficient vehicle for the student assistance program. Although this group should include, on a rotating basis, at least one member of the child study team, it is not meant to replace or overtake the responsibilities of the child study team itself.

The student assistance team meets regularly to discuss identified at-risk students and formulate intervention strategies to assist these students. The student assistance team considers all referrals presented as per the accepted referral procedure. The team can be cochaired by the principal and student assistance counselor or other counseling personnel or it may rotate the leadership on a regular basis among all the members.

## Forming the Team

The core of the student assistance team should consist of professional staff that have no classroom responsibilities and can be summoned on an emergency basis at any time during the school day. The principal, nurse, and counseling personnel (whether student assistance, guidance, or child study team members) can be the designated and permanent members of the core team that handles crisis situations of an acute and immediate nature (i.e., suicide, child abuse, drug/alcohol abuse, criminal activity, etc.).

The makeup of the remainder of the student assistance team should be flexible, changing to include some or all of the following staff as their expertise relates to the nature of the referral: the referring teacher, the speech and language specialist, the reading and math specialists and/or master teachers for the grade level of the student being discussed. The presence of the learning disabilities/teacher consultant from the child study team can be a powerful addition to this group. It is also important to include personnel who have a considerable opportunity to interact with the general school population and have relatively easy access to a wide variety of student-related data.

## The Role of the Student Assistance Team

In general, a student assistance team can be responsible for the following activities:

- serving as a child advocacy vehicle by identifying potentially high-risk students
- generating grade-level surveys to assess each student's potential for dysfunctional and/or destructive behavior
- reviewing referrals for individual students and generating a data collection to supplement the referral information
- scheduling and conducting meeting to discuss referrals, review supporting data, and plan interventions for students identified as at risk
- involving the parent in both the intervention planning and strategies

- providing training for students, staff, and parents in identified areas of concern
- generating specific programs, support groups, and other types of projects to address identified needs among the student population
- providing appropriate referrals to outside agencies and providers for families who require them
- responding to crisis
- acting as a prereferral mechanism, much like a school resource committee, to provide interventions for students who may be considered for referral to the special education child study team

Note: The role of the student assistance team may take many forms, but one it should avoid is that of a treatment provider or therapist. These tasks are best left to professionals outside the educational setting.

### Responsibilities of Team Members

#### Principal

- cochairs the team
- provides pertinent data regarding administrative contact with the student and parents
- gives administrative sanction to intervention plans that the student assistance team develops
- monitors the performance of team members, i.e., the role of members during meetings and accountability for team assignments

#### Student Assistance Counselor or Guidance Counselor

- cochairs the team
- is responsible for all recordkeeping and statistics for team
- notifies members of meetings, provides agendas of students and topics to be discussed, coordinates the data collection, monitors the intervention plan, screens students to be discussed, performs classroom observations, and provides interventions as determined by the team

#### School Nurse

- provides pertinent health information about the referred student
- acts as a contact person when required

*Teaching Staff*

- provides information about referred students
- contributes behavioral and educational strategies to assist referred students
- assists the student assistance counselor in the data collection among professional staff
- confers with staff who deal with the referred student to assist in modifying curriculum or implementing strategies
- is assigned, on a rotating basis, as a contact person to work with a particular student and his/her teachers or parents for the purpose of monitoring the success of the intervention plan; daily contact with the student and positive reinforcement for brief periods of time may be included as part of these responsibilities
- updates the student assistance team on the progress of the student, as necessary

*Child Study Team*

Note: Recognizing the extent of the child study team's responsibilities with regard to the provision of services to the school's educationally handicapped students, their participation in the activities of the student assistance team should be included on a rotating basis. Ideally, one member of the team should attend these meetings.

- assist the team in formulating prereferral interventions
- become familiar with cases that may eventually be referred to the child study team for possible evaluation
- perform classroom observations and review samples of the academic work of children referred to the student assistance team
- participate in intervention strategies as unilaterally decided by the team

**Training of the Student Assistance Team**

Ideally, once a team has been formed, its members should receive some type of training so they may effectively carry out their duties. In addition to understanding the dynamics that arise in any group of people, members need to become familiar with information related to the at-risk student. An outside consultant can structure a training designed to teach this information along with communication skills while creating opportunities for the group to become cohesive. An ideal training usually is held off-site for a period of three to five days. Follow-up sessions should be provided during the year to reinforce the initial training and dispense additional information according to the needs of the team and the kinds of cases they have seen. Team training should include:

- the roles and responsibilities of the team
- developing a team purpose while recognizing individual styles
- identifying at-risk students by understanding behavioral signs and symptoms (in-depth exploration of the more prevalent reasons for referral)
- data collection and assessment process
- techniques for screening students
- formulating intervention plans for students
- strategies to work with parents
- accessing community resources
- maintaining appropriate confidentiality
- monitoring and follow-up support for interventions
- ongoing care and maintenance of the team

A successful training program is something the group can draw from throughout the year when difficulties arise. The training can help student assistance teams to remain mindful that they will be pursuing a common purpose despite their individual styles. A group member who monopolizes meeting time or who is negligent in carrying out tasks is more easily dealt with when members have been trained for such situations.

## CONFIDENTIALITY

Few issues generate as much controversy, misunderstanding, and resentment in a school setting as does the question of confidentiality. Seen as a legal and ethical responsibility among mental health professionals, confidentiality in the small, familial atmosphere of an elementary school is seen as a divisive element that separates the elite from the rank and file. Considerable effort should be made to have a shared consensus and acceptance among staff of what confidentiality is and how it will be maintained.

Any nonschool related information disclosed by a student to a staff member can be shared with parents or other professional staff on a need to know basis. Disclosures of such information must occur if there is potential danger to the student or others. The most common automatic disclosures happen when the child appears to be a danger to him/herself or others. Reports of child abuse, suicidal thoughts, or dangerous drug/alcohol use are always reported to the parents and/or child protection agency, regardless of the wishes of the child.

In the high school setting, the preponderance of students disclosing information about their drug and alcohol use requires careful adherence to CFR 42, the federal confidentiality regulations that make criminal the sharing of such information with others without the written consent of the student. Good counseling practice extends that principle to nondrug related information that is shared within the protection of a counseling session.

In the elementary school setting, it often becomes necessary for confidential information to be shared with selected staff on a need to know basis if the child is to get the proper assistance. However, elementary-age students cannot give informed consent for such matters since their capacity for understanding is considerably less than that of their older counterparts. Parents of elementary students then become the givers of consent for the sharing of sensitive information.

Confidentiality is necessary for the protection of the privacy of children and their families. Staff who become indignant when their direct questions about sensitive issues regarding a student are not freely discussed should realize that this protective action is extended to all children, including their own wherever they may attend school. However, those staff that deal directly with high-risk students have a need to know how to respond to the manifestations of the child's particular problem. The best rule of thumb is to obtain the parent's permission to share information with these staff members. Casual disclosures of information learned through the activities of the student assistance program should never take place, especially as topics of discussion in the faculty room.

When the school has made a referral to an outside agency and the parents wish the school to work in tandem with that outside provider, a release of information must be signed by the parents. The outside provider must also obtain the parent's signature in order to release any information to the school. The parents will usually designate one person (most often a counselor and/or the principal) to receive this information. Because the student assistance team comes under the umbrella of student assistance and the bounds of confidentiality, the information may be disseminated there on a need to know basis. The parents should give direct consent for any other personnel to receive the information (e.g., the student's classroom teacher if it is necessary).

### Staff Orientation to the Student Assistance Team

All staff will be involved in some way with the student assistance team whether through referring a student or becoming involved in the data collection, intervention, or monitoring process. A staff meeting with an accompanying handout that explains the purposes and the responsibilities of the team is a necessary step in helping all staff begin to see the program as an integral part of the school.

Staff should understand that the team's purpose is to assist in identifying students who are in need of assistance and to provide interventions. The team can connect students with the outside resources they need, enlighten and support parents through this process, and serve as a consultative resource for the professional staff who deal with these students. Staff orientation should also include a discussion of reasonable expectations of the team and staff's role in their activities.

### Care and Maintenance of the Student Assistance Team

Ideally, teams initially attend a three- to five-day training and return with a great deal of enthusiasm and ideas about getting the program started. As the weeks go by, the daily pressures of their regular duties may become overwhelming when coupled with the emotionally draining demands of the team. Especially frustrating is the failure to bring about tangible changes in the behaviors of chronic referrals. The displeasure these team members experience from their colleagues because of these perceived failures becomes stressful.

Within the team, resentment may exist because of perceptions that the tasks are unequally distributed or that some members do not contribute to the group. One person may be seen as too dominant. The entire team may feel overburdened with a large number of referrals and be fast approaching burnout.

Provisions need to be made to talk about these issues without fear that an open and honest discussion will destroy the team. Previous training can prepare a group to communicate and confront effectively, without hidden agendas. The team itself can use its problem-solving skills to address the issues that are causing stress among its members. Regular meetings specifically for this purpose, wherein no students are discussed, are a necessary component for the continued success of the team.

### Scheduling the Activities of the Student Assistance Team

Elementary school days are structured very differently from those at the secondary level. Whereas at the secondary level it might be possible to find several teachers who share the same nonteaching period, it becomes a scheduling nightmare at the elementary level.

There are several ways a principal can schedule team meetings so that all members can be present. The easiest and least expensive way is to find common nonteaching periods among those with classroom responsibilities. At the elementary level, this seems to become a near impossibility. Another alternative is to schedule meetings either before or after school or during lunch. There are tremendous drawbacks to holding meetings at those times. The staff is tired after school, preoccupied before school, and need time to recharge during lunch. If meetings are infrequent, these times might prove acceptable. However, another option that seems to work in elementary schools is to schedule meetings once or twice per month and hire a substitute to provide coverage for those teachers who need to attend the meeting. Several students can be scheduled for the meeting day, while the substitute relieves each teacher when his/her particular student is slated to be discussed.

## EMPLOYING A STUDENT ASSISTANCE COUNSELOR AND/OR COORDINATOR

Many school districts have created a position that can develop and lead a comprehensive student assistance program K−12. The state of New Jersey has provided funding and training assistance for over 120 school districts to create these programs. Most of these districts have hired a ''student assistance coordinator'' to oversee the operations of the program and provide direct services to students; these coordinators often report directly to a central office administrator.

As the programs grew in size and scope, additional student assistance staff, called counselors, were hired to provide direct service at various school sites. Although the programs were originally designed to target drugs and alcohol, many became more broad-based, encompassing other areas of risk that interfered with a student's successful educational experience. To that end, individuals with experience in the provision of varied human services, as well as drug and alcohol intervention, were sought.

What follow are sample job descriptions of a student assistance coordinator and a student assistance counselor. It is important to remain mindful of the fact that student assistance personnel do not act in isolation from the other resources of the school. The integration of all aspects of the school experience is what makes a student assistance program so powerful.

---

### Student Assistance Coordinator

1. Develops and coordinates a comprehensive student assistance program for grades K–12.
2. Coordinates and monitors the activities of the student assistance teams and core teams at each school site.
3. Serves as a supervisor to student assistance counselors in their provision of direct services to students.
4. Provides educational programs for staff, students, and parents regarding the prevention, identification, and treatment of substance abuse.
5. Assists in the implementation of the K–12 health curriculum, *Here's Looking at You, 2000*.
6. Develops a comprehensive assessment program that measures the effectiveness of the prevention, identification, and interventions of students at risk.
7. Serves as a resource to staff, parents, and students who may require professional services outside the educational setting.
8. Provides training for staff in the identification and assessment of students at risk.
9. Attends and participates in professional meetings at the local, state, and national levels that are involved in improving student assistance programs.
10. Consults with members of the child study team in designing and carrying out the prereferral process.
11. Establishes a materials center, including a professional library on student assistance.
12. Devises and maintains such records and reports as are necessary to the successful execution of the position.
13. Assists in the development of grant applications to local, state, and federal agencies.
14. Participates in district and community advisory committees and task forces.

---

## Student Assistance Counselor

1. Demonstrates a real and personal interest in student concerns and aspirations.
2. Provides individual and group counseling where needed to address student problems that involve substance abuse, as well as academic, social, and emotional issues.
3. Coordinates the activities of the student assistance team members at their assigned sites.
4. Assists teachers in addressing issues that involve the home environment.
5. Maintains a flexible work schedule to meet the needs of the parent community (some evening hours required).
6. Provides developmental activities/groups which include values clarification, problem-solving techniques, and social skills and provides to staff in-service in these areas.
7. Provides prereferral interventions for students who may be considered for referral to special education.
8. Develops and implements plans for the periodic crises facing the children in their schools in order to minimize the negative effects of such problems.
9. Assists in implementing programs that will maximize the climate for learning.
10. Develops, implements, and facilitates parent training and support programs.
11. Serves as the school liaison for outside agencies.
12. Identifies situations that are risks for learning.
13. Meets with students to assess their counseling needs and make appropriate recommendations.
14. Assists the principal in maintaining accurate records of referred students and intervention and monitoring actions.
15. Remains one half hour after the regular staff hours, during which time parent conferences, support groups, etc., may be scheduled.
16. Keeps written records and statistics of students referred to the student assistance team and forwards monthly summaries of these records to the student assistance coordinator.
17. Monitors the process by which staff members refer students, and generates additional referrals where needed.
18. Acts as a consultant for staff members to assist them in implementing strategies for referred students at risk.
19. Acts as a resource for parents, both through individual conferences and parent training programs.
20. Provides short-term supportive counseling on an individual basis for identified students as needed.
21. Maintains the standard of confidentiality in all endeavors that so require.

## HOW IT WORKS—THE ELEMENTARY STUDENT ASSISTANCE TEAM IN ACTION

Ellen, grade one, is referred to the student assistance team by her classroom teacher. Areas of concern listed on the referral form included limited time spent on task, difficulty following directions, incomplete and missing assignments, and social isolation from her peers.

The team schedules Ellen's referral for its next meeting later that week and begins the data collection in the following manner. The learning consultant from the child study team observes Ellen during class and at recess and lunch. Samples of Ellen's academic work are selected by the referring teacher and brought to the meeting. The student assistance counselor has a brief meeting with Ellen to gain a sense of her perceptions of school, her attitude toward achievement, and her peer and family relations. The nurse reviews Ellen's health records to assess the extent of physical complaints and previous health milestones. The principal, though finding no disciplinary reports, reviews the notes he had made about a previous phone contact with Ellen's mother. She had complained about Ellen's classroom teacher, saying that the work required in class was too difficult for first graders. A conference between Ellen's mother and teacher had appeared to resolve the issue at that time. Ellen, however, continues to perform sporadically.

The reading specialist is assigned to contact Ellen's other teachers (music, art, physical education, etc.) to determine if her behavior is consistent in all settings. With the exception of art class in which Ellen is quite productive, she is experiencing difficulties in all of her special subjects.

### Team Meeting

After all of the information is reviewed, several hypotheses are put forth. Ellen is somewhat younger than her classmates. This might explain a developmental lag in her socialization skills. Her ability to complete visual assignments in art class, while being unable to follow verbal directions in other classes, gives rise to the suspicion that Ellen might have a hearing problem. The learning consultant's preliminary assessment of samples of Ellen's academic work does not suggest the presence of a perceptual problem. Ellen's comprehension of tasks seems age-appropriate.

The following intervention plan is proposed:

(*1*) Ellen's parents will be brought in to work with the team to address Ellen's difficulties and to give consent to the strategies as listed here.

(*2*) The speech/language specialist will do a preliminary assessment of Ellen's skills.

(*3*) The nurse will arrange for a hearing test for Ellen.

(*4*) Ellen will be placed in a primary-level social skills group. This group, facilitated by the student assistance counselor, runs continuously in six-week cycles.

(*5*) Ellen will have as many of her instructions as possible given to her visually. She will be encouraged to continue her artistic projects and be given special projects in the classroom that will showcase this ability in the hopes of raising her self-esteem and involving her more positively in school.

(*6*) The reading specialist is assigned as Ellen's contact person, as this is her turn in the rotation. She will monitor the plan and keep the team abreast of the effectiveness of their proposed strategies and arrange for additional meetings should alternate strategies be indicated.

## SUMMARY

This chapter dealt with the planning and design of a formal mechanism to identify and assist students in the elementary school setting who are impeded in the learning process by various developmental lags and situational deficits. By using the existing resources of available staff and a designated interdisciplinary team, a student assistance program that can also provide primary prevention activities can be researched, designed, and adopted.

# CHAPTER 6

# The Referral Process

## STAFF REFERRAL

TEACHING STAFF ARE usually the first to identify potential problems among the student population. Confusion may exist, however, about what kinds of problems require a formal referral to the student assistance team. Many times teachers are reluctant to make such a referral for fear that it will negatively reflect upon their effectiveness in the classroom.

Grade-level meetings that take place within an atmosphere of collegiality can do much to alleviate these fears. Teachers can review their rosters of students and discuss specific behaviors and areas of concern. Ideas can be shared about strategies that were successful in similar situations. Decisions can be reached in a safe and supportive way about making appropriate referrals to the student assistance team for difficult, resistant, or puzzling cases.

Training can provide professional staff with the information to identify students who require assistance and intervention. A comprehensive referral form listing observable behaviors that may be indicators of risk is an excellent tool for raising the awareness of professional staff for early identification. In reviewing such a form, staff should be instructed to look for patterns of these behaviors, or sudden and acute changes in a previous behavior.

All staff should have these referral checklists (i.e., the referral forms) at their disposal so they may continually review the listings of observable behaviors that signal concern. This allows them to look for and note specific behaviors as they consider the appropriateness of a referral for children in their charge.

Part of the referral form should allow for narrative expansion on steps the staff member has already taken to address the concern. All referrals should include some mention of the *strengths* of the child, so as to balance the primary focus on negative behaviors and provide a more integrated profile. Figure 4 shows a sample referral form specifically designed for elementary-age children.

In order to ensure that students at risk become identified at the earliest opportunity, and to ensure that these students' needs are responded to in a timely fashion, professional staff should be familiar with the procedures necessary to make a thorough referral to the student assistance team. A list of possible reasons for referral helps staff determine ap-

---

Student _____ Grade _____ Room _____

Referring Teacher/Staff _____ Date _____

(Please complete this form and return to the student assistance counselor's office in a sealed envelope or hand delivered.)

What is your area of concern for this student? _____

_____

Have you contacted the parents? _____ Outcome? _____

_____

Please check the behaviors that appear to be patterns rather than isolated incidents.

__ Does not complete academic tasks        __ Violent/aggressive behavior
__ Withdrawn, isolated from peers          __ Difficulty following directions
__ Physical complaints, visits to nurse    __ Frustration, cries easily
__ Exaggerates, lies, makes excuses        __ Difficulty concentrating
__ Poor hygiene, unkempt appearance        __ Absenteeism, tardiness
__ Unprepared for school                   __ Profane language, gestures
__ Teased/rejected by peers                __ Perfectionistic
__ Exhibits anxiety/worry                  __ Bullying behavior
__ Sexually precocious                     __ Daydreams/fantasizes
__ Excessive physical activity/movement    __ Does not participate in class activities
__ Inappropriate/bizarre behavior

Describe _____

Actions already taken _____

_____

What are the *strengths* and *interests* of the child? _____

_____

Comments: _____

_____

_____

Thank you for your referral. You will be contacted regarding the status of this case as soon as possible.

*Figure 4. Student Assistance Program—Elementary Referral Form.*

propriate concerns for the student assistance team to address and allows for uniform reporting in data collection for the program. The following reasons might be included on this list:

- academic performance
- grief/loss
- social/emotional difficulties
- suspected AODA (alcohol or other drug affected)
- eating disorders
- attendance problems
- suspected abuse/neglect
- truancy
- suicide discussed
- disruptive classroom conduct
- family dysfunction
- antisocial behavior
- stress
- socialization difficulties
- chronic illness
- enuresis

Some programs encourage teachers to complete these forms and forward them in sealed envelopes to the interdisciplinary team representative. However, if staff are encouraged to hand deliver the form to a member of the team, productive discussion about the child can begin immediately. Information can be clarified by a one-to-one exchange.

Figure 5 is a flow chart of how the referral moves through the program (Ogden and Germinario, 1988).

Teachers should understand the entire procedure for referring a student to the student assistance program.

## SAMPLE STAFF REFERRAL PROCEDURES

(*1*) If a student's work is deteriorating, or if a change in social patterns is observed, then it is expected that the classroom teacher will take action, such as:
- calling the parents
- talking to colleagues, e.g., other teachers of the student
- speaking to the student to ascertain what may be causing the change
- varying teaching techniques
- discussing the student at a grade-level meeting

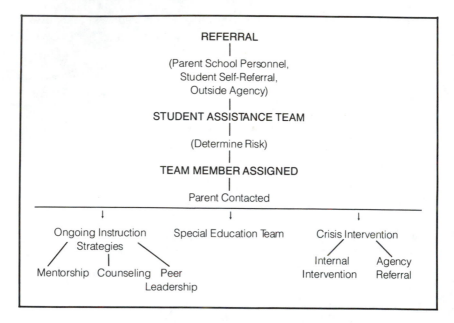

***Figure 5.*** *Elementary School Student Assistance Program Organization.*

(*2*) After the above actions have been tried and the causes for concern persist, the staff member completes the referral form and sends or brings it to the student assistance counselor. (If the situation is one that requires immediate attention, i.e., suicidal ideation, the principal should be notified who, in turn, will convene the core team for response.)

(*3*) The student assistance counselor or team member meets with referring teacher and screens the student. Suggestions may be offered to the teacher at that time to address the student's concerns.

(*4*) If a referral to the team is indicated, the student will be placed on the team agenda, data collection will begin, and the referring teacher will participate in the team meeting. Parents are also involved in this process.

(*5*) The case is presented at the team meeting. Data are reviewed, a preliminary assessment is made, an intervention plan is developed, and a contact person is assigned to the student. Follow-up and monitoring continue in subsequent meetings.

## PARENT REFERRAL

Parents should receive notice that the school is prepared to offer assistance to their children in a variety of social-emotional areas. They should be encouraged to make use of these services and instructed how to access them. This information can be relayed by mailings, PTA meetings, and public relations programs. (Figure 6 is a sample parent letter sent out at the beginning of each year.)

Should parents wish to refer their children to the student assistance

---

Dear Parents and Students,

All students will have access to short-term individual and group counseling and other supportive services from the student assistance specialist in their school. The specialist at (name of school) is (name of specialist), who will be in your school two and one-half days each week on (specify days).

Support services at the elementary level are designed to be preventative. If children's concerns are dealt with at the earliest opportunity, we believe that more serious problems can be averted in later years. Many of the activities of the student assistance program encourage the development of social skills, self-esteem, problem solving, and coping with difficult life situations. These are accomplished through the use of support groups, classroom activities, individual counseling, and cross-age interactions.

When an area of difficulty has been identified, whether academic, behavioral, or social-emotional, the student assistance team in your building will work with parents to plan intervention strategies to assist children and provide outside referral information as needed.

Students and/or parents may contact (name of specialist) directly or through the principal or classroom teacher. The specialist's number is (specify number). Please call if you have any questions or concerns.

The student assistance program will also be providing a series of parent workshops throughout the year on a variety of topics. These workshops are scheduled in the school calendar that was sent to all district parents.

We look forward to a happy and productive year together.

Sincerely,


(Principal or Student Assistance Coordinator)

---

*Figure 6. Sample Parent Letter.*

team, the contact person, i.e., the classroom teacher or nurse, can complete a referral form with the help of the parent's responses as to the behaviors they are observing. Sometimes parents become prematurely concerned about their child's difficulties and request a referral to the child study team before any interventions have been tried. Although a parent's written request for such a referral is always honored, alternatives should be presented to them for their consideration. The student assistance team can be the mechanism for explaining this process and providing strategies to assist the student should the parent so decide.

## SELF AND PEER REFERRAL

If a student assistance counselor or guidance counselor is employed by the school, it is important that he/she becomes the visible presence that children can associate with getting help. Time should be provided at the beginning of the school year for them to facilitate introductory activities in all classes. Children should understand what types of concerns are appropriate for self or peer referral and how they should go about asking for help. An effective, nonthreatening method is for the counselor to provide a special "mailbox" for students wishing to be seen. The sign may read: "If you need to speak with me, please leave a note with your name and classroom teacher on it. I will call for you when it is a good time to meet. Thank you, Ms. Glover."

This approach also prevents students from using requests to see the counselor as a means of avoiding schoolwork or classtime. Ideally, the counselor can find an opportune time to arrange for a meeting that would be least disruptive to the student's other responsibilities. Counselor and teacher should continue to reinforce the kinds of concerns that are appropriate for a session request, while at the same time providing other sources of help in more minor concerns. Naturally, any child who is distraught and unable to concentrate or any child involved in an emergency situation would be seen immediately.

## INFORMATION GATHERING

Before any students who have been referred to the interdisciplinary team are discussed, a data collection process should be completed. A total profile of the student should be compiled so that a timely and effective assessment can be made when the team meets. The members of the team should bring the following information to the student assistance meeting:

- observations of the student in various settings
- health records/frequency and nature of visits to nurse
- administrative records (discipline, attendance, tardiness)
- academic records
- teacher feedback (other than the referring teacher)
- parental input/contacts
- information from student interview/screening

Ideally, the referring teacher will be present to work with the team to review the initial referral, make an assessment, and decide upon an intervention plan.

## INTERDISCIPLINARY ASSESSMENT

When reviewing information at the student assistance team meeting, it is important that the members of that team avoid hastily drawn conclusions in their assessment of the situation. Often, previous perceptions of the child in question may color their taking a fresh look at the problem. It is not always an easy task to ascertain a child's motivation or to identify the causes behind problem behaviors. Some of the questions that should be raised during assessment are:

- Does the referring problem occur for that child in all settings and in all interactions? If not, what patterns emerge?
- Are there situational factors or life events that coincided with the onset of the referring problem?
- Does a review of the child's past performance in earlier years reflect a marked change?
- How does the presenting problem fit into the psycho-social development of the child?
- What are the child's perceptions of and reactions to the presenting problem?

The following is a case study provided to give a clearer picture of what referral and assessment might look like in an elementary setting.

## HOW IT WORKS—A CASE STUDY: DANNY G., GRADE FIVE

Mrs. Hill, Danny's teacher, brings a completed referral form for Danny to the student assistance counselor, Ms. Glover. She reports that Danny is continually defiant and seems able to get the class to support him whenever he decides to disrupt the lesson. Ms. Glover suggests they review the checklist together to ensure that she has a clear picture of what is happening. The following behaviors are checked:

- often does not complete assignments
- unprepared for class
- calls out
- engages in physical contact with other students
- easily angered
- argumentative
- distorts the truth

Mrs. Hill notes that although Danny does not complete his assignments, he always does fairly well when tested on materials from most subjects. When asked what actions have already been taken, Mrs. Hill reports various disciplinary actions she has imposed (time out in another teacher's room, after-school detention, and being sent to the principal's office). Danny's parents have also been contacted. They report that Danny displays none of these behaviors at home, but they would speak with him about his school behavior. None of these actions proved effective.

Ms. Glover thanks Mrs. Hill for her referral and tells her that she will soon receive a notice to attend the student assistance team meeting in which Danny will be discussed. Ms. Glover then visits Danny's other teachers, mentioning that Danny has been referred to the team. She asks for any behavioral observations they can contribute. (The data collector should refrain from mentioning the reason for referral both in the interests of confidentiality and to preserve objectivity.)

Ms. Glover asks the reading and mathematics specialists, both members of the team, to review Danny's academic records for presentation at the team meeting. The school psychologist, who attends student assistance team meetings on a rotating basis with the social worker and learning consultant, is asked to observe Danny in a number of settings and prepare an informal report. Notices of Danny's referral are sent to the other members of the student assistance team. According to procedure, the principal and nurse bring the attendance, disciplinary, and health records.

Since Danny's parents have recently been contacted by Mrs. Hill, and have reported that the behaviors only occur in school, Ms. Glover decides to wait until after the meeting to contact them. However, she does conduct an interview with Danny a few days before the meeting. Although Danny comes to her office, he does not speak freely and answers her questions with one-word responses. He repeatedly asks if he may return to class and says, as he walks out the door, ''There's nothing wrong with me. The teachers here are stupid.''

At the student assistance team meeting, the principal and Ms. Glover elicit reports from the various staff present about Danny's performance and behavior. A profile begins to emerge of a boy who seems to alternate periods of staying on task and behaving appropriately with responding angrily to the slightest correction or criticism. This pattern seems to occur in all of his classes, with Danny responding to his male science and physical education teachers in a less hostile way.

Academically, Danny passes his tests and sporadically completes enough assignments so that all his grades are in the C range. No learning problems or academic deficiencies are currently indicated.

Danny is larger than many of his peers and his physical aggressiveness often leads to frequent altercations on the bus and the playground. His classmates are beginning to avoid him. Outside of school, Danny plays football for a local team that his father coaches. Danny is often featured by the town newspaper as a star player.

After further discussion, the team formulates the results of their assessment. It is determined that Danny's primary problem is social/emotional. More specifically, his impulsiveness, lack of emotional control, hypersensitivity to criticism, and poor social interactions will be the targets of the intervention plan.

Danny's case will be continued at the close of Chapter 7.

## SUMMARY

This chapter dealt with the steps to be taken for the early identification of students experiencing difficulty in the educational setting. Once identified, students are referred to the student assistance team, which will include parents and staff involved with the student in the data collection, assessment, and intervention process. Procedures for such actions should be clearly delineated and understood by the professional staff.

# CHAPTER 7

# *Intervention*

## IN-HOUSE INTERVENTION

HOW CAN INTERVENTIONS in an elementary school be structured using available personnel, whether or not there is access to counselors?

No school district, regardless of the amount of educational and psychological specialists it employs, can offer varied and effective in-house interventions if the following conditions are not created and maintained:

*1. Teaching staff must play a key role in the formulation and implementation of intervention plans for at-risk students.*

This may sound rudimentary, but it is essential to address the resistance that an already overburdened staff may express when asked to take on additional tasks. The finest intervention plan is doomed to fail if the cooperation of teaching staff is not secured. Teachers need to be encouraged to take ownership for the problems of at-risk students by including them in decisions about the children they refer. Teachers resent being handed a list of intervention strategies that was formulated by an interdisciplinary team of ''experts'' that did not include the person who sees the child most frequently.

*2. Administrative personnel must provide support for proposed changes in program and encourage experimental activities to address identified needs in the student population.*

Often, if several children have been identified as experiencing difficulty because of a similar problem (e.g., poor social skills or living with a substance-abusing parent) it is necessary for the building administrator to assist the staff in the creation of a strategy (e.g., the development of a teaching unit to address the concern or the formulation of a support group for these children). Once that strategy is agreed upon, the administrator must assist with the structuring and scheduling of time during the school day or as an extracurricular endeavor. Parental involvement and/or approval for interventions is more easily gained when there is active administrative support for the activity.

*3. Professional staff who provide counseling and other direct support services to students and parents should possess the appropriate clinical training.*

There is a temptation to overutilize certain teaching staff for services for which they may not be adequately prepared. Most often, these are the staff members who relate well to the students, frequently volunteer for special projects, and are most generous with their time. Although such staff may prove invaluable in facilitating support and informational groups and in providing individual mentoring for at-risk students, there is a danger of their taking on the role of a therapist without having professional training. It is the responsibility of supervisory personnel to ensure that teaching staff who take part in interventions for students understand the limits of their role and know when and how to refer to an outside professional.

## STRATEGIES FOR IN-HOUSE INTERVENTION

As previously stated, existing resources in the school can be used in the provision of creative and effective strategies to address the at-risk elementary student. The following activities and approaches can be modified to suit the particular needs and resources of any school.

### Mentoring

The dissolution of the stability of the nuclear family for many of today's children has created a situation in which the school is expected to fill what were once familial roles. Students are coming to school with added responsibilities. With the increase in the number of single-parent families and those in which both parents are employed outside the home, many children begin and end their days without the supervision of a parent. More and more responsibilities become part of a student's day; often they are in charge of minding younger siblings. If parents return home in the early evening, the children are alone or in the care of another adult or a latchkey program for several hours following the close of school.

Providing students such as these or other students from dysfunctional families with an adult mentor in the school setting can prove to be an effective strategy for intervention. Students should be selected based upon their need for support in academic and/or emotional areas.

Mentors should be chosen from those staff who volunteer and agree to undergo training. Much harm can be done to children who become involved in a program that is sporadic, poorly planned, and staffed with people who do not understand their roles; it is not enough to have caring adults whose intentions are good but who lack the skills to effectively serve as mentors.

Matching a student with a teacher/mentor should be carefully done so that temperaments, common interests, and the particular skills of the mentor are considered. The teacher/mentors should be provided with an orientation so they may understand the goals of the program and their commitment to the students. The parents and their children who will participate should also be provided with an orientation so they will have realistic expectations for the program.

Mentors will provide support and positive role modeling for students. In addition, mentors should be aware of the three stages that relationships with these students typically go through:

(*1*) The honeymoon period is characterized by the politeness and good will present in the initial exchanges between students and mentors. The novelty of the situation and the newness of the relationship fosters this misleading stage.

(*2*) The testing period is characterized by the introduction of negative behaviors of the student to the relationship. Meetings are missed, the adult is avoided, contract terms are not adhered to, and the student verbalizes not wanting to continue the relationship. *This is the critical stage at which most mentoring and "Big Brother, Big Sister" programs fail.* Adults need to understand that this is a necessary phase that must be undergone in order to develop a more meaningful relationship with the student. It is an opportunity for adults to provide guidance and confrontation in a supportive way so that the students understand that they will not be abandoned because of their behavior or failure to conform. If the pair can successfully weather this phase, they can move to the most powerful stage.

(3) The influencing period is characterized by a true feeling of trust between the pair, and thus the possibility for real influence. The mentoring relationship is one that must develop over time and model for the student how healthy relationships in the future should be formed.

Mentors should be able to maintain some sense of detachment lest they become professional enablers to these students. The aim is to increase the students' self-esteem so they may be empowered to do things for themselves, not to have others do things for them.

After the training of the adults is completed, and the students and their parents have attended orientation, some sort of structured bonding experience should be designed for the mentoring adult/student pairs. Ideally, this could include a Saturday off-site retreat, or an after-school activity at which introductions and bonding activities can take place. However, some of these activities may also be done at the school site if off-site training is not possible.

*Mentoring Activities*

When the mentoring pairs have completed this initial experience, the ongoing, daily support can be structured to work effectively in the time and space restraints of the school setting. The pairs can begin and/or end each day with a short supportive meeting, or have periods within the school day to meet. Lunching together and structured recreational activities both alone and with other mentoring pairs could be scheduled. Most important, however, is the inclusion of periodic support and follow-up meetings with the adult mentors. They will be needed for additional guidance and support in handling these challenging children.

*Mentoring Closure*

All participants in the mentoring program should understand the limitations of such a program. One way to ensure that students do not become overly dependent upon such adult, intensive support is to set clear limits on the amount of time such a program will run. A volunteer teacher will feel less overwhelmed by the commitment and responsibility needed to undertake this program if his/her commitment is limited to a school semester or school year. A healthy relationship can still develop in that amount of time while empowering the students to continue on their own with the coping skills they have learned.

### Specialized Groups/Group Counseling

Support groups are effective and efficient means to address identified concerns among the student population. Group work enables counselors/and or teachers to impact a greater number of students in the same amount of time as would an individual session. In addition to providing a forum for nonjudgmental discussion of sensitive issues, one of the greatest benefits of group work is the establishment of a support network of peers for the students involved. Existing problems such as divorce or death of a parent, or a parent's substance abuse, can be discussed in a safe environment wherein students can take comfort in learning that their problems are shared by others.

What kind of groups can be facilitated at the elementary level?

The types of concerns that most often adversely affect the elementary student's school experience are as follows:

- death of a parent
- limited social skills
- parent's divorce
- multicultural differences
- parent's substance use
- attending a new school
- ineffective anger management
- child abuse/neglect
- low self-esteem
- being retained
- poor organizational/work habits
- learning disabilities

When children are identified as being affected by these concerns, groups can be designed to help these students cope. Teachers, nurses, and counselors can be trained to facilitate these groups if these factors are considered:

- These groups are not meant to be therapeutic. They will supply information, teach new skills, and provide students with a forum to work with other students with similar concerns.

- The groups should be designed to have a finite number of meetings (one meeting a week for eight to twelve weeks is common) in which a clear progression of topics and/or skills are delineated for each week.
- Group facilitators should have ongoing supervision to assist in handling situations that arise within the group and to monitor the adherence to the proposed aims of the sessions.

### Individual Counseling

Long-term therapy should not be offered in the academic setting. This cannot be overstressed. Many parents, when informed of the existence of a student assistance program in their child's school, expect the counselors to provide every service their child may need. Although many services can be provided, it is important that parents and school personnel remain mindful that the program exists in an *educational* setting.

Individual counseling provided by student assistance counselors should be limited to *short-term supportive counseling*. Eight to ten individual sessions with an elementary student should be the time frame within which counseling goals are structured. If it appears, either at the onset or during the short-term counseling, that the student needs more frequent, more intensive individual counseling, a referral to an outside practitioner must be considered.

### Classroom Strategies

Often, teachers can implement various plans and techniques that can address problematic behavior in identified students. The interdisciplinary team can be invaluable in making classroom observations and working with the teacher to design strategies to help identified children.

Behavior modification is a systematic way of bringing about changes in observable behavior. The focus must be on behavior that is specific, observed, counted, and evaluated rather than on global behaviors or underlying causes. It is best understood by realizing that behavior can be changed by altering the consequences, rewards, or outcomes that follow the behavior.

Behavior modification techniques, when well-planned and consistently carried out, can be quite effective in changing behavior. Most commonly, reward systems work well with elementary students to help motivate them to complete work, keep them on task in a timely fashion, and discourage negative behaviors that may disrupt the class.

Children should be included in an appropriate manner when designing a plan to modify their behavior. Too often students are treated as guinea pigs, subject to generic behavioral plans that may have ill effects due to some particular sensitivity possessed by the child. For instance, a student who is being ostracized by classmates may suffer more from other students being aware of his/her particular behavioral plan than a student who is well-integrated socially. Thus, any time the student fails to obtain a reward, he/she is subject to the disapproval of peers on top of his/her own disappointment.

The first step in designing a behavior modification plan is to isolate and define specific desirable behaviors for reinforcement or undesirable behaviors for reduction. Every effort should be made to break the behaviors down to specific, small actions so that a child can readily see some success. Also, only two or three behaviors should be targeted so as not to overwhelm the child. Then a reinforcer should be selected with the specific student in mind. Some reinforcers might be:

- verbal praise
- material rewards and tokens
- social reinforcers
- games and special privileges
- extra grade points
- homework passes (one day without)
- special notes to parents

When possible, it is a good idea to work with parents in setting up and implementing these plans. The person implementing the plan should also devise a system to count and record the behavior and commit to being consistent and faithful to the plan. The reinforcers should also be consistently given according to the plan.

Administrators can provide training for classroom teachers in behavior modification by introducing specific techniques and providing guidelines for choosing activities to solve specific classroom problems. Training should include a basic overview and time for discussion and practice. Follow-up sessions should be designed to discuss the implemented techniques to troubleshoot or modify activities for greater effectiveness.

## Bibliotherapy

A simple and effective method of helping children and parents deal with life traumas or specific behavioral problems is to provide them with books and instructional pamphlets designed to explain such issues in an age-appropriate way. Parents and children often take comfort in the fact that they are not alone in what they are experiencing, and there are suggested ways of coping that have proved successful for others in similar situations.

A good source of books is the *Bookfinder 4: When Kids Need Books*, a listing of annotations of children's literature that addresses their needs and problems (ages two and older). The collection is published by American Guidance Associates, Circle Pines, Minnesota and edited by Sharon Spredemann Dreyer.

Libraries can provide lists of books on specific topics. Bookstores are also sources of therapeutic readings. Waldenbooks offers a listing called "Tough Topics" that is furnished upon request.

## Prereferral Interventions

The term, prereferral, is usually understood within the context of referrals to special education for children who may be educationally handicapped. It is customary for children to be afforded a number of educational and behavioral interventions before a decision to refer to the child study team is reached. For example, in the state of New Jersey, parents must receive in writing any such strategies that were tried with their child before any request for a child study team evaluation can be made.

Schools need to have formal mechanisms in place for identifying and intervening with children before referring them to the child study team. The student assistance team, which often includes members of the child study team, can be that mechanism. The committee, which is charged with providing interventions for nonhandicapped students experiencing difficulties in their regular classes, can also serve. This committee is also charged with developing recommendations for new programs and services to expand the existing strategies available for children.

It is important to note, however, that the student assistance team must remain aware of the constraints and mandates of the area of special education, and continually take direction from the child study team in these matters. Parent requests for referrals to the child study team are always honored. Care should be taken not to delay inappropriately the referral of a child who clearly needs an educational evaluation in order to get the help he/she needs. The workings of the student assistance team, including efforts to provide prereferral interventions, should not impede a timely and appropriate referral to the child study team.

When preparing a referral to the child study team, a listing of the prereferral strategies should be included with the letter notifying parents of the intent to refer. The person preparing the letter can select the strategies that were used and thus provide parents with a written record of prereferral activities.

### Crisis Interventions

Anticipating that crises may occur at any time, provisions need to be made for safe and appropriate responses for the protection and well-being of students, staff, and parents. Specific sections of this book will deal with death at school, suicide, and child abuse, in which crisis intervention is specific and carried out through the leadership of the building core team. Any other crises can be addressed by using the basic format of a core team's immediate assembly, formulation of a specific plan, and continued monitoring and adjustment of that plan.

## HOW IT WORKS—A CASE STUDY:
## DANNY G., GRADE FIVE (CONTINUED)

In the previous chapter on referral, Danny had been discussed during the student assistance team meeting. It was determined that Danny's primary presenting problem was social/emotional. More specifically, his impulsivity, lack of emotional control, hypersensitivity to criticism, and poor social interactions would be the targets of the intervention plan.

The following plan is proposed:

(1) Danny's parents will be enlisted to support the behavioral interventions taking place at school, as they had reported no problems at home. They will be told that Danny's current behavior at school will

not be tolerated and must be addressed. They will be asked to provide rewards, reinforcements, and consequences for Danny's behavior at school.

(2) Rather than globally trying to change Danny's entire style of inter-action with others, two specific behaviors are targeted to address:
 • his disruption of class by loudly exclaiming his displeasure at the lesson and his refusal to participate
 • his physical aggressiveness, most specifically his initiation of fights with other children

(3) A behavior modification plan will be devised aimed at the elimina-tion of these two behaviors and the acquisition and reinforcement of other more positive and constructive behaviors.

(4) To that end, several options were considered. In order to foster more kindness and sensitivity in Danny, it is suggested that he work with younger students. However, others on the team have seen him interact with youngsters on the playground; he is cruel and self-ag-grandizing with the children. The team feels he is not ready to be placed in such a situation.

Instead, because Danny appears to have a talent for sports, the team decided to enlist the support of one of the junior high school students as a positive role model. They will make arrangements for Danny and the student to spend some time together working on both sports and academics. It is felt that this student will exert a positive influence on Danny, showing him how a person can be powerful and productive without having to hurt people.

(5) Danny's teacher will facilitate the daily behavioral plan in the classroom while a designated member of the team agrees to monitor Danny during lunch and recess. The principal will impose conse-quences as needed should Danny continue to fight with others or disrupt class.

(6) Danny will meet with the student assistance counselor on a weekly basis while the plan is in effect in an effort to work on anger management techniques with Danny and explore his self-esteem issues.

### Outcome

Danny's meeting with the junior high school student goes well. As anticipated, Danny is anxious to display his sports prowess, but is somewhat in awe of the skills of the older boy. It is extremely powerful for Danny to see how the older boy does not taunt Danny for not being as skilled as he, and how he offers praise for the skills that Danny does have and offers suggestions for how he can improve.

Danny finds that he understands math better than the older student. At first, Danny is most ungracious about his advantage, but gradually he begins sharing hints of how to attack different kinds of math tasks, and praising the older boy when it appears to help.

Danny's behavior in the class begins to improve as he is able to vent his frustrations to the counselor about his hating being told what to do. Danny's father continues to have a strong, demanding manner with his son, but Danny comes to realize that he can develop his own style of dealing with people and still enjoy the things he does. The reward system devised by the teacher gives Danny something to shoot for, and although he has many reversions to old behaviors, he gradually begins to develop more positive interactions with others.

## SUMMARY

This chapter dealt with specific in-house interventions that might be used for identified students in the elementary school setting. The creative use of existing resources can provide the student assistance team with a wide and varied selection of strategies to recommend for referred students.

# CHAPTER 8

# Enlisting the Aid of the Community

## OUTSIDE REFERRALS

BECAUSE SCHOOLS ARE educational institutions, every effort should be made to refute the notion that they should provide in-depth treatment for their students and their families. This is not to say that school personnel should not advocate for children or that they cannot provide services that, although therapeutic in nature, will ultimately improve the student's educational experience. Part of this responsibility is to furnish information to students and their families about the assistance that outside agencies can provide.

When discussing such referrals with parents, school personnel should always make it clear that the decision to follow through with a referral ultimately lies with the parents. *Schools cannot mandate that families pursue the assistance of outside service providers.* There are three exceptions to this statement. They are concerned with the areas of child abuse/neglect, suicidal risk, and substance abuse. The first two areas are dealt with in separate sections of this book.

## SUBSTANCE ABUSE

Every district should have in place a clear set of policies and procedures for the prevention of substance abuse. State and federal statutes and guidelines for such procedures should be carefully reviewed and integrated into such documents because of the growing amount of litigation regarding this issue.

The following are some generic guidelines to keep in mind when developing and implementing a philosophy, policy, and procedures regarding substance abuse in the schools:

Educate the staff, students, and community on the "hold harmless" statute in your particular state. New Jersey's (from N.J.S. 18A:40A) reads as follows:

". . . *No action of any kind in any court* of competent jurisdiction shall lie against any teaching staff member, including a substance awareness coordinator, any school nurse or other educational personnel . . . or any other officer or agent of the board of education . . . because of any action taken by virtue of the provisions of this act, *provided the skill and care given is that ordinarily required and exercised* by other such teaching staff members, nurses, educational personnel . . ." (emphasis added)

". . . Any teacher, guidance counselor, school psychologist, school nurse, substance awareness coordinator or other educational personnel . . . *who in good faith* reports a pupil to the principal or his designee . . . or school nurse in an attempt to help such pupil cure his abuse of substances . . . *shall not be liable in civil damages* as a result of making such report." (emphasis added)

A copy should be distributed to each member of your professional and support staff.

Take the position, and emphasize it in your policy, that the removal of a student from school who has been proven to be under the influence of alcohol, steroids, and/or controlled dangerous substances is for his/her own safety and that of the other students. The legal aspect is one that you may need to emphasize for more resistant parents, but try the first approach in your contact meeting. A parent who is convinced that your primary goal is to help his/her child will be a tremendous asset to that process.

This same position should also be taken in cases where there is suspicion that the student is under the influence. Your policy should always include parent notification as well as the need for parents to immediately remove the student from school and accompany the student to a physician. The examination should include the collection of a urine sample and a physical examination which results in a written document which states whether the student is or is not physically and mentally able to return to school. When the results of the chemical screen are positive (and this may take three to five days to receive, during which the student should have been attending school if the physician's report so indicated) the student should be removed from school and the procedures for a positive result should begin.

Have clear and consistent consequences for a positive chemical screen. There is no benefit for students, their families, the general perceptions of staff, the student body, or the community if substance abuse is treated as a "lightweight" matter. It is also vital that every student, no matter what the extenuating circumstances (e.g., honor student status, athlete, troubled home) be subject to the same consequences. This is not to say that there should not be incentives for cooperating with the intervention plan. For example, a first positive screen may result in a three to five day out-of-school suspension and an exclusion from all extracurricular activities for a period of at least three weeks. School personnel, most notably the interdisciplinary team, should then be given the discretion to extend or terminate that exclusion based upon the compliance of the student to the terms of the intervention plan.

Know your outside substance abuse assessment and treatment providers. During the suspension period, mandate that the student and his/her parents meet with your student assistance counselor or other counseling personnel to make an initial assessment and recommendations for the student's reentry. If you have no such staff, meet with the parents to refer for an outside assessment that should provide you with the same information. Your interdisciplinary team should be greatly involved in this process to ensure the student's successful reentry into school.

Become familiar with confidentiality regulations by reading CFR 42. This is specific to the area of drug and alcohol interventions and comes under scrutiny with regularity in cases where families bring legal action against the school for infringement of their child's individual rights.

When dealing with elementary-age students, do not summarily rule out the possibility of these younger children being at risk for abuse of substances. According to the National Health Statistics, the *average* age for initial experimentation is nine and one-half years.

Design a strong prevention component for your program. Research has shown that delaying the onset of experimentation results in less likelihood of addiction. Prevention programs should be a required part of the curriculum.

## MAKING APPROPRIATE REFERRALS TO OUTSIDE AGENCIES

### Accessing Resources

In cases where a family may benefit from family therapy or individual therapy for their child, school personnel should give at least three names of providers for the parents to choose from. The student assistance program can develop a *resource list* for this purpose. Names of providers, fees, insurance coverage, specializations, and informal notations of satisfaction from other parents can be included and passed on to parents to assist them in choosing a therapist. Many agencies and providers offer technical assistance and training for staff and parents. This also helps to establish a trusting relationship for future referrals.

### Providing Appropriate Information

When making a referral to a therapist or treatment facility, it is important and ethical to mention if you are making a "blind" referral. If no one on staff has visited a treatment facility, you should make that fact known to the family. It is preferable to know your referral sources so that you can provide parents with the most complete information. Ultimately, they will make the choice; however, your expertise in assisting them in this endeavor will be most welcome when they are trying to deal with a stressful situation.

### Confidentiality and Release of Information

If the parents wish for the school to work in tandem with the outside provider in exchanging information about the student, a form authorizing release of information must be signed by the parents. The outside provider must also obtain the parent's signature in order to release any information to the school. The parents will usually designate one person (usually a counselor and/or the principal) to receive this information. Because the interdisciplinary team comes under the umbrella of student assistance, the information may be disseminated there on a need to know basis. The parents should give direct consent for any other personnel to receive the information (e.g., the student's classroom teacher if it is necessary).

## PARENTAL INVOLVEMENT AND SUPPORT

Parents should be seen as partners in the educational process of their children. To that end, they can be encouraged to be active participants in the child's intellectual and social development. Many parents need information about how to go about reinforcing what children are learning in school while providing opportunities for moral and social growth outside the school.

### Parent Training

Individual conferences are an excellent means for educators and counseling personnel to work together with parents to assist their children. Time constraints do not make it possible to provide all the assistance they may need. One way to reach many parents effectively and economically is by offering parent workshops on specific topics. A survey can be devised so that all parents can be polled on which topics they believe are most in need of information. Experts both from within the school and from outside agencies can be enlisted to design workshops around the most requested topics. These workshops should be flexibly scheduled so some offerings are held in the evening and some during the day.

A workshop for parents of kindergarten and first grade students is essential for setting up appropriate expectations for the educational process while providing support for parents who may be feeling overwhelmed by the newness of the situation.

The workshop series, which might be titled "The Right Start," could be composed of four sessions that encompassed the following areas:

- separation and transition
- age-appropriate expectations
- social development
- troubleshooting and problem solving

Discussing these topics and providing current and accurate information can prove extremely helpful to parents. Workshops also have the added bonus of providing opportunities for parents to speak with other parents who may be experiencing many of the same concerns.

Regardless of what kinds of offerings the student assistance program provides for parents, the good will that is cultivated among the parent community is an invaluable asset to the climate of the school.

### Resistant Parents

Few aspects of the intervention process are more frustrating than when a parent does not become involved in assisting his/her child. This behavior can be characterized by resistance, avoidance, hostility, and sabotage. When designing workshops or support programs for parents, staff often acknowledge that the resistant parent, whose child appears to be in need of assistance, is not likely to attend. Nor is the parent responsive to requests for individual conferences, regardless of which school official has made the request.

It becomes difficult not to inadvertently penalize the student for his parents' lack of cooperation. Care must be taken that ultimatums issued by the school do not do harm to the child or forever distance parents from any productive communication.

Attempts can be made to engage parents by involving them in both the assessment and formation of an intervention plan for their child. Skilled educators and counselors can present problematic behavior without seeming to place blame on a parent prone to defensive responses. However, the best efforts to engage parents can still result in their noninvolvement. Some suggestions for the resistant parent are:

- Create a crisis. Some parents only respond when the status quo is upset. This is often enough to mobilize a family into action. Suspending a student and requiring the parents to appear for his/her reentry can provide an opportunity for a face-to-face meeting.
- Threaten to legally refer the parents for the student's nonattendance at school. When extended efforts to bring the child in have been made without success this threat may result in the child's return to school.
- Offer assistance to the parents for other issues that may be interfering with their ability to cope and respond to school requests regarding the child.
- Enlist the support of the child protection agency when the parents have refused help for their child or will not take the necessary steps to obtain it.
- Try to identify more supportive parents of other children who know these parents and might exert some influence. They might share how the school had helped their children and what the school accomplished in their particular situations.

Dysfunctional family systems hold fast to their ways of relating to each other and the world, regardless of the harm they inflict. Engaging such families in outside therapy is a motivational goal that the student assistance team can and should pursue.

## SUMMARY

This chapter dealt with enlisting the support and involvement of the community, both among parents and among agencies and providers of treatment for families and children. Guidelines for identifying resources, making appropriate referrals, and providing parent training were reviewed.

# PART THREE

# IMPEDIMENTS TO LEARNING: HIGH-RISK SITUATIONS FOR THE ELEMENTARY STUDENT

**REGARDLESS OF THE** degree of foresight and precautions taken by a school, some children will remain at high risk because of life events, familial factors, and social/emotional dysfunction. However, children who are affected by these kinds of circumstances, such as child abuse, death of a parent, or living in a chemically dependent home, should not be "written off" as the chronic failures of the future. Educators can effectively help these children to understand the nature of their difficulty and can empower them with the necessary skills to cope in age-appropriate ways. In order to accomplish this task, educators must first become knowledgeable about the particular problem, examine their own attitudes on the subject, and develop strategies and interventions to assist these children and their families.

**THE FOLLOWING CHAPTERS** examine in depth a number of areas that are frequently identified as sources of risk for elementary school students. Each chapter provides information about the extent of the problem, its behavioral manifestations, and suggestions for help. At the close of each chapter, a detailed case study is included to help illustrate how an intervention plan can be designed and carried out. Additional resources on many of these topics are included in a special section of this book.

# CHAPTER 9

# Bullies and Victims

IT IS IMPOSSIBLE to ensure an optimal school climate for all students when the element of fear is a daily factor for them. It is estimated that 10 percent of all school children are habitual victims of the 7 to 8 percent of children who are bullies (Olweus, 1984). The National Association of Secondary School Principals surveyed middle school students in 1983. These students cited the behavior of other students, including bullying, vandalizing, and stealing, as their greatest worry while at school. Teachers in elementary and middle school grades regularly identify about 12 percent of all boys as often harassing or oppressing others in physical or psychological ways (Hoover and Hazlet, 1991).

School professionals who handle this problem by tolerating it, playing it down, or ignoring incidents of bullying send unspoken messages to the entire student body. The failure to take a decisive stand to intervene in the victim's behalf makes a strong statement about the worth of those students. There is evidence that students who were bullied continue to associate pain and anxiety with any peer interaction in adulthood (Gilmartin, 1987). By making clear, consistent interventions with bullying incidents, school officials send a positive message about the worth of all students and the need for the school climate to be safe and nurturing.

## WHO IS A BULLY?

A bully is a child who oppresses or harasses another child in a physical or psychological way. Bullies are usually male, but some female bullies do exist. They try to control their fellow students with aggressive behavior to relieve their own feelings of low self-esteem (Elkind and Weiner, 1978). Observable behaviors include starting fights, teasing,

97

answering back, verbal threats, and damage to or confiscation of material possessions of the victim.

Surprisingly, bully children are more popular than children who are randomly aggressive, possibly because they choose their victims from among weak and unpopular students and relate well to the majority of other students. The existing pattern of teachers intervening for these unpopular students with inconsistent frequency may be sending a tacit message that it is socially acceptable to victimize certain children (Hoover and Hazler, 1991).

There are certain factors that facilitate the development of bully behavior. It is a behavior that can be learned from the home, the peer group, or the school. Because it is learned, it can be unlearned. Although bullying has as its basis a poor self-concept, other life experiences strongly feed into developing this behavior. Harsh, physical punishment teaches children that it is acceptable to hit others. Bullies model this hitting with those smaller and weaker than they. Bullies also model aggressive behavior enacted between their parents, learning quickly that the stronger one ''wins'' and gets his/her way.

Bullies see the world as more negative than positive because the messages they receive from others focus always on what they are doing that is wrong. They rarely receive positive comments. By expecting this pattern from others, bullies take the offensive and attack without provocation. They automatically assume that hostility exists everywhere.

## WHO IS A VICTIM?

Children who are consistently the object of aggressive or oppressive acts by other children are the characteristic victims in a school setting. Some of these children are passive, in that they seem to do nothing to invite these attacks and cannot or will not defend themselves. The other type of victim often provokes attacks by annoying and teasing others, and unsuccessfully fights back when attacked.

One commonality among victim children is their lack of good and meaningful friendships at school. These children are often overprotected by their parents and have not had the opportunity to develop social and coping skills of their own. Victim children are unpopular with others and are often overrepresented among special education populations.

## THE SCHOOL'S ROLE IN ADDRESSING
## BULLYING AND VICTIMIZATION

School personnel should make a strong commitment to change these behaviors by forming alliances with parents of both types of children to address the problem at home and in school. Special training for parents and teachers can be provided to help them understand the nature of the problem. They should be encouraged to give clear, consistent messages about the unacceptability of bullying behavior while increasing positive messages to bullying children. Specific social skills training for both bullying and victim children can be reviewed by parents and teachers and provided in the school setting while being reinforced at home. Because bullying behavior often begins as early as two years of age, early intervention is essential.

Discipline practices for bullying incidents should emphasize positive restitution rather than detentions. Children who are caught bullying should be expected to apologize, demonstrate the correct behavior, and spend some time working with younger students or those students needing help and assistance.

An ideal climate for supporting kindness and fairness in dealing with others should include a discipline system that both teachers and students develop and enforce. Conflict mediation and resolution that is implemented by trained students is an excellent deterrent to reduce incidents of bullying. Bullies will be less likely to repeat such an incident when their behavior has been judged unacceptable by children in their classroom.

Cooperative learning and goal structuring reinforces improved social integration among classmates. Specific classroom activities aimed at sensitizing students to the dynamics of bullying and victimization can be facilitated by counseling personnel and/or classroom teachers. These activities can be extracted from such publications as *Getting Along with Others* by Nancy F. Jackson, Dr. Donald A. Jackson, and Cathy Monroe (Research Press), and the series from American Guidance Services on Developing Self and Others (DUSO) social skills and PUMSY self-esteem curricula.

## HOW IT WORKS—A CASE STUDY:
## BULLYING AND VICTIMIZATION

The principal receives a call from the father of Matt, a fourth grader. Matt is reportedly being harassed in the classroom, at recess and on the school bus by a classmate, Frank. Matt's father says that these incidents are daily occurrences and although his wife has spoken to the teacher on several occasions, they have not been satisfactorily addressed by the school. The principal obtains further information from the parent about the specific behaviors that have been occurring and promises to call back after investigating the situation.

The principal speaks to the classroom teacher who reports that she has been aware of these incidents for some time but her efforts to intervene have not been successful. She expresses frustration and impatience with Matt, the victim, because he is "constantly coming to her about Frank, even for things like having his pencil taken or being called a 'baby.'" She also states that Matt is extremely unpopular with the other children, while Frank, although sometimes cruel, is able to socialize successfully with his classmates. The principal realizes he needs to address the problem in both an immediate and a long-range fashion.

He asks the teacher to attend an interdisciplinary meeting that he will call for the following morning before school. The teacher is instructed to prepare a brief listing of the kinds of incidents that have taken place and how they have been handled. He assures the teacher that he understands how difficult these situations are and hopes that the interdisciplinary team can strategize with her to assist her in the future. In the meantime, the principal asks to speak to both boys at separate times in his office. He sends for Matt first. The principal also asks that the school counselor be present for the interview.

### Meeting with the Students

Matt reports to the principal and counselor that Frank is constantly harassing him and that the teacher never "does anything" when he reports these incidents. He claims he hates coming to school and only has good days when Frank is absent. The counselor concentrates on validating Matt's feelings of frustration and getting a general sense of his overall coping skills. She questions him about his other friends, what is positive in his life, what kinds of things he does when he feels hurt or sad, and what his general self-image is like. The principal concentrates on obtaining specific data about the kinds of incidents and the times and places they occur, the frequency and how they are handled. At the close of the interview, the principal assures Matt that the incidents he reported will not be tolerated in the school and that steps will be taken to stop them. Matt is asked to see the counselor at an appointed time the following day to further explore some responses to Frank and to talk more about how he is feeling. Matt is instructed to continue to inform his teacher about the incidents during the following day, and to meet with the principal at the close of the day to discuss how the day has progressed.

Next the principal and counselor meet with Frank who reports that Matt is exaggerating and that most times Matt initiates the conflicts. The counselor gives the same general screening to Frank as she did to Matt. The principal also tries to obtain specifics from Frank about any past incidents. The message to Frank at the close of the interview is that the alleged behaviors will not be tolerated in the school from anyone. Frank is asked to see the counselor during the school day for a continued session. He is also asked to report to the principal at the close of the day to review how the day has progressed.

The principal calls Matt's father, informs him of the actions taken, and promises to meet and work with him after the interdisciplinary team has met to address the problem. Frank's parents are also called and informed of the situation. They are asked to attend a meeting with school personnel following the interdisciplinary meeting.

### *The Following Morning—The Team Meeting*

The principal opens the meeting with a brief overview of the situation. He explains that the goal of the meeting will be twofold: first, the team is charged with developing a plan to assist the students, the teacher, and the parents to stop the bullying incidents; second, he asks for the team's input and assistance in assessing and addressing the overall problem of bullying and victimization throughout the school.

The boys' teacher gives particular details about the incidents and previous strategies and responses tried. A pattern emerges of inconsistent responses, vague consequences, and a current response pattern of impatience with Matt's reports leading to ignoring the reports and not dealing with Frank in any way. The ignoring of Matt's complaints has lessened the amount of time taken from instruction but is sending a message to Matt, Frank, and the other students that the behavior is acceptable and they are on their own to handle it. As a result, the bullying behavior has escalated, with other children now beginning to victimize Matt.

The nurse reports on her dealings with Matt, who sometimes comes to her with physical complaints during recess, a time when most of the incidents are taking place. Although he never appears ill, she spends the time speaking with him about a variety of subjects.

The counselor shares her assessments of both boys and their current behavioral profiles. She feels that Matt can benefit from social skills training and self-esteem work. Frank needs to be redirected and reassured in other ways, and needs to have clearcut consequences for his behavior.

The team offers to work with the teacher in implementing the following strategies:

- Every incident of bullying must be responded to in a clear, consistent manner. Whenever such an incident can be substantiated, Frank will be asked to apologize to Matt and asked to demonstrate or describe the appropriate behavior. Frank will then need to make some positive restitution in the form of service to younger children or other children needing academic or athletic assistance.
- The counselor will design a series of lessons that she and the teacher will facilitate to sensitize the class to bullying and victimization.
- Frank needs to be reinforced daily whenever he is seen doing something positive, kind, and/or helpful.
- Matt also needs positive reinforcement daily whenever he is observed handling a situation on his own, accomplishing tasks, and engaging in making friends.
- Cooperative learning activities will be designed to foster greater and more positive interaction among the students.
- Since other students were identified as bullies or victims from other classes, the counselor will design social skills groups to address deficiencies particular to this group.
- The teacher will meet with the parents of both boys and the counselor to provide them with strategies for home that will reinforce what is being done at school.

## *The Parent Meetings*

Frank's parents discuss his behavior at home, which seems to be consistent with his bullying behavior in school. The counselor explains the dynamics of this behavior and informs the parents of the strategies the school will be using. It is suggested that the parents try the following strategies at home:

- They should be as positive with Frank as possible, looking for at least five positive comments to counteract the one negative comment they may need to say when addressing negative behavior.
- When they observe Frank bullying another child, they should stop it immediately and have Frank practice the appropriate behavior a few times. For example, if Frank is yelling at his sister to get something for him, and hitting her when she refuses, he could model asking nicely for her to get the object, and also model getting it for himself.
- Supervision is key to the plan's success. Corrections cannot be made if the incidents are not observed. The parents are asked to instruct caretakers of the procedures to be followed in their absence.
- Use of physical punishment should be eliminated. Privileges can be revoked, tasks around the home can be assigned, or Frank may be required to help other children in the home or the neighborhood.
- They should be aware of the behavior they model for Frank. If they yell or bully each other, Frank will internalize this method as the proper one for interaction.
- They should continue to communicate with the school to monitor Frank's progress in both settings.

### Meeting with Matt's Parents

Matt's parents spoke about his shyness and his difficulty making friends. The counselor explained the dynamics of children who become victims and provided them with the following strategies to use at home:

- If the parent can be present during a bullying incident, prepare the child in advance to say ''stop bothering me'' to the bully and then walk away.
- They should give Matt more opportunities to handle tasks without assistance. They should be aware of their behavior in possibly trying to overprotect and shelter Matt from many tasks he needs to learn to cope with. The social skills training he receives in school can be reinforced at home, doing role-plays for behavior alternatives in difficult situations.
- They should encourage Matt to engage in activities in which he

will excel and also to experiment with new and challenging activities.

- Matt should be encouraged to make new friends, starting out with concentrating on one student and gradually expanding this circle.

### Long-Range Solutions from the School

The team works with the principal in getting feedback from students and teachers about the extent of the bullying problem. The percentages affected are consistent with national norms. The survey process succeeds in raising awareness of the problem.

Teachers are provided with an in-service on the dynamics of the problem and strategies to use in the classroom. The idea of using students for conflict mediation is explored. Clear, consistent disciplinary responses for bullying incidents are adopted, including mechanisms for allowing positive restitution to take place. Classroom activities to reduce and/or prevent this problem are discussed. Several grade-level groups are formed to teach social skills to identified bullies and victims.

## SUMMARY

It is estimated that 10 percent of all school children are victims of the 7 to 8 percent that are bullies. These patterns, gone unchecked, often adversely affect school performance and healthy adult interactions. Schools should provide adequate supervision and quick, consistent intervention in bullying incidents. Positive restitution, social skills training, and parent/teacher consultations are some of the methods used to help establish a climate in which the worth of every student is foremost and incidents of oppression will not be tolerated.

# CHAPTER 10

# Children of Substance Abusers (COSAs)

TWELVE MILLION SCHOOL-AGED children live in homes where a parent is a chemically dependent substance abuser. These children suffer from a variety of physical and emotional maladies. COSAs go to the hospital at a greater rate and stay longer than other children. Their diagnoses usually fall within the categories of mental disorders and substance abuse (study by the Children of Alcoholics Foundation, 1990).

COSAs are overrepresented among learning-disabled populations, in part due to fetal alcohol and/or drug effects. They constitute 50 percent of all physical and sexual abuse cases, and 70 percent of all adolescents in drug and alcohol treatment (Black, 1981). The behaviors of these children can range from perfectionistic and driven, to impulsive and oppositional. Chronic absenteeism often interferes with their ability to succeed academically.

Research indicates that children of alcoholics are more likely than other children to become chemically dependent. Sons of alcoholics are five times more likely than other males to become alcoholic, daughters twice as likely (see *Children Are People*).

The dysfunction of the home, often characterized by erratic parenting, interferes with the child's normal developmental processes. Because young children do not question their parent's authority, there is an acceptance of the home situation as normal. Many children receive spoken and unspoken messages from their parents not to speak about what goes on in the home to outsiders. They quickly learn not to trust and not to feel. This numbness is a protection against the daily pain of living with a chemically dependent parent. Teachers who understand the dynamics of the chemically dependent family will be better able to identify these children in their classes.

## IDENTIFYING CHILDREN OF SUBSTANCE ABUSERS

The following behaviors, adapted from *Broken Bottles, Broken Dreams*, Deutsch, 1982, may characterize these children. In identification, it is important to consider the development of patterns of behavior rather than an isolated incident.

- poor or erratic attendance
- frequent physical complaints and visits to the nurse
- morning tardiness, especially on Mondays
- inappropriate fear about the possibility of parents being contacted
- equating any drinking with being drunk or being alcoholic
- perfectionistic and/or compulsive behavior
- difficulty concentrating, hyperactivity
- sudden emotional outbursts, crying, temper tantrums
- regression (thumbsucking, enuresis, elective mutism)
- friendlessness, isolation, withdrawn behavior
- a passive child becoming active or focused during drug/alcohol lessons
- lingering after instruction concerning drug/alcohol to ask unrelated questions
- signs of abuse or neglect

Although many of the other behaviors may have their causes in other problems, signs of abuse or neglect frequently go hand in hand with a chemically dependent home.

## WHAT ARE THE DEFENSES (SURVIVOR ROLES) THAT CHILDREN OF SUBSTANCE ABUSERS ADOPT?

Since children often mistakenly take blame for what is wrong in the family, some may feel that if they behaved better or accomplished more, then the parent would stop drinking. Others engage in acting out behaviors so as to take the focus off the drinking behavior of the parent.

Their confusion and isolation from being in such families are dealt with using a variety of defenses that characterize the roles they take on to survive. By taking on these roles, the focus is removed from the chemically dependent parent . . . about whose disease the entire family is in denial. These traits and coping mechanisms are the result of living in *unpredictable and highly stressful homes*. Such children come to believe that these abnormal situations are normal. Some of the roles children from chemically dependent homes take on are the hero child, the scapegoat child, the class clown or mascot, and the lost child. We will look at each of these roles individually.

### The Hero Child

Usually the oldest child in the family, he/she is also characterized as an overachiever. Other characteristics:

- overresponsible, often behaves with adult mannerisms
- achieves in every area undertaken, but appears to gain little satisfaction from successes; is despondent or angry when losing or when receiving less than perfect grades
- compulsive about volunteering, completing tasks in a perfectionistic way, and being organized and dependable
- appears overly serious and unable to have fun
- is manipulating and controlling

Without help, the hero child as an adult becomes addicted to work and may "burn out" and drop out of the mainstream altogether. Such an adult remains rigid and controlling in his/her interpersonal relationships and continues to take responsibility for everything, delegate nothing, and become exhausted and depressed.

In dealing with hero children, a teacher should:

- Give them attention when they are not achieving or are undertaking a task they may not do well.
- Limit the amount of times they are chosen when they volunteer, and avoid constantly giving them leadership roles.
- Do not continually praise them for their achievements. Validate them for their kindness, their sense of fairness, and their humor (on the rare occasions it is displayed).

### The Scapegoat Child

These children are among the most difficult to manage in a classroom. They create an uproar whenever possible to mirror what takes place at home. Their behavior results in the refocusing of the blame and anger from the alcoholic parents to themselves, thus keeping the denial about the disease at status quo. Other characteristics are:

- defiance and confrontational behavior, especially with authority
- disruptive, engaging in risk-taking behavior
- identifying strongly with peers and not adults or parents
- early chemical use

Without help, these children will continue a pattern of disruption and delinquency. In dealing with a scapegoat child, a teacher should do the following.

- Give clear messages about inappropriate behavior, set limits, and impose consequences.
- Attempt to see the hurt in the child that lies beneath the angry and destructive behavior.
- Teach decision-making skills by allowing the child to connect action with consequence. Praise the child for responsible choices.
- Praise kind actions, achievement, and adherence to rules.
- Provide opportunities for these children to work with younger children where they can exhibit constructive, helping behaviors without threat.

### The Class Clown or Mascot

These children often go unidentified as ones who live in a chemically dependent home because they seem so charming and happy. They take great pains to smooth over any conflicts by using their humor and charm, as they do at home. Other characteristics include:

- attempts to be funny at inappropriate times; uses pranks and practical jokes to get attention
- may appear somewhat hyperactive
- seeks approval by listening to others, offering warmth, and avoiding conflict by denying his/her own needs
- has difficulty being taken seriously and disguises his/her feelings with jokes

Without help, these children never learn to handle stress effectively. By repressing all conflict, they may develop physical ailments. Their interpersonal relationships cannot develop on a mature level. In dealing with a mascot child, a teacher can do the following.

- Provide opportunities for the child to take responsibility for important projects.

- Avoid encouraging clowning by not laughing when child is joking at inappropriate times.
- Praise the child for responsible action or nonjoking behavior. (Be patient when child responds with a joke. He/she does not know how to express feelings.)

### The Lost Child

Often overlooked, this child is withdrawn, quiet, and lives in a world filled with fantasy. The child deals with the family and with life by withdrawing into a private state, being fearful to interact and pursue needs and wants. Other characteristics include:

- compliant, but will not initiate action
- isolated and aloof
- creative and imaginative
- sometimes overweight
- speaks little in class, will rarely take a key role in projects

Without help these children have poor interpersonal relationships and often turn to drugs and alcohol to further escape their pain. In dealing with lost children, teachers can do the following.

- Introduce touch slowly, and respect their space.
- Try to encourage peer relationships, but slowly, starting with a pairing with one child to build confidence before including the child in larger groups.
- Refrain from always letting the child ''off the hook'' when asking for participants.
- Praise efforts the child makes to identify and pursue needs.

## THE SCHOOL'S ROLE IN HELPING CHILDREN OF SUBSTANCE ABUSERS

### Staff Training

Children who have been identified as having a parent who is actively abusing drugs or alcohol can be helped, to some extent, in the school setting. In-servicing of staff about the extent of the problem, the nature of the disease of chemical dependency, identification of children, and ways to cope with their behaviors should be provided. The following information, in addition to the previous material in this chapter, can be included in the training.

(*1*) Follow through after the child asks for help. The child has taken a considerable risk in confiding in someone outside the home. Know the helping professionals within and outside the school to whom the child may be referred. Help the child to identify all of the sympathetic adults who are in his/her life (grandparents, other relatives, friends) who might be able to help.

(*2*) Remain mindful of cultural differences that will influence how the child will be best helped.

(*3*) Assist the child in placing focus on his/her own needs and wants.

(*4*) Praise and provide affirmations that he/she may not have received in the home.

(*5*) Monitor reactions of embarrassment or discomfort when a child confides such information. Criticisms of parents or excessive sympathy should be avoided.

(*6*) Build trust with the child by keeping the information confidential unless it must be shared with another professional to ensure the child's safety.

(*7*) *Do not break promises or appointments with the child.* The child will be unable to develop trust if inconsistencies continue.

### Curriculum

A logical tool in helping to provide children with the correct information about chemical dependency is the drug and alcohol component of a health curriculum. Lessons about family alcoholism often result in self-disclosure from students who have not understood their home situation until the class discussion provided clarification. The *Here's Looking at You 2000* curriculum, a comprehensive K–12 curriculum, is comprised of the elements of information, social skills, and bonding. Many of the lessons deal in an age-appropriate fashion with chemical dependency in the family. One of the duties of the school is to provide information and reassurance to children who live in these homes that the dependency is a disease that they did not cause, they cannot cure, but they can learn to live with by learning how to take care of themselves.

### Support Groups

As with other support groups, children who participate learn that they are not alone in their problem and that there is a safe place to ask questions, discuss their situation, and examine their feelings. Support, not therapy, should be the group goal in an educational setting. If the child's nonabusing parent is aware of the child's disclosure and wishes the child to participate, progress can be made toward helping the family take steps to obtain help for its members. Many times, however, these children do not wish their parents to know that they have disclosed the ''family secret'' at school. In these cases, if counseling personnel determine that the parents would not approve of the child participating in such a group, school officials still have an obligation to the child to provide these services. These parents can be informed that their children have the opportunity to participate in a support group to develop better interpersonal skills and personal growth. Some problematic behaviors of the child that have been observed may be cited as the reason for his/her proposed inclusion in the group.

Noncounseling personnel can be trained to facilitate these groups or cofacilitate them with a counselor. An excellent model for designing these groups is the *Children Are People* materials from Health Communications, Inc., Deerfield Beach, Florida.

Hopefully, the groups will provide an adult role model to interact with children in a healthy way. Children will be provided with information about the disease, how they adopt their roles and how they are affected. They will learn how to focus on themselves and channel their feelings into doing positive things for themselves. They will have their experiences validated, and begin to be able to separate their parents from the drinking/drugging behavior.

Sessions should be held at a prearranged time and place and children should know how many sessions will be held (twelve sessions are recommended). Materials, such as art supplies, toys, etc., should be in abundance. These children are children of need. Food of some sort should also play a part in the nurturing nature of the group. Provisions should be made at group closure to monitor the children with continued informal support and referrals, if age-appropriate, to Alateen, a self-help group for children affected by another's drinking.

### Individual Counseling and Referral

Sometimes students may not be ready to participate in a group setting. Individual work can be done to provide the same type of information that the children in the group are receiving. Naturally, if the counselor determines that a child requires more intensive treatment, in either a group or individual setting, appropriate referrals must be made.

### Professional Enabling: What Not to Do

Many caring professionals, in their efforts to assist children from such situations, create more problems by making special allowances for their behavior. Many of these children engage in acting-out and risk-taking behaviors that need to be related to clear and consistent consequences. Staff members who feel compassion for children because of the chaos of their home situations sometimes allow students to continue unacceptable behavior rather than impose a consequence that may add extra stress to the children's lives. This is professional enabling. Staff that look the other way when they suspect chemical experimentation, perhaps because they are uncomfortable in handling the situation, are also guilty of professional enabling.

Staff need to understand that compassion takes many forms. Children can be validated as people whose worth is measured apart from their behaviors, for which they should be held accountable. Reasonable demands for all children with a consistent set of rules and consequences help to establish a standard of healthy normalcy with authority.

## HOW IT WORKS—A CASE STUDY: CHILD OF AN ALCOHOLIC

Eddie, grade four, has been referred to the student assistance team because of his oppositional behavior, his refusal to complete assignments, and his continuing series of disciplinary incidents at school-related activities. Before the team meeting, team members gather data from all of his teachers about his behavior. Eddie's mother is contacted by the student assistance counselor, informed that he has been referred to the team and asked for input as to his behavior at home. His mother reports no problem at home, but feels he is "somewhat headstrong, like his father." The counselor tells Eddie's mother that she will be called following the meeting when all the information has been reviewed.

The counselor also meets with Eddie to do a screening for his perceptions of what is happening both at school and at home, and to do an initial assessment of his coping skills. Eddie is angry about having to speak to the counselor, and responds to many of his questions with, "It doesn't matter" and "Just suspend me, I don't care." When asked about how things are going at home, Eddie says, "None of your business." The counselor tells Eddie that he and others want to help, that sometimes children who do the things that Eddie does are in pain about something else. If Eddie wishes to talk with him at any other time, the counselor will welcome it. Eddie leaves the room saying, "Don't hold your breath."

### Team Meeting #1

Eddie's teacher gives a brief overview of the kinds of things she is seeing in the classroom and on the playground. Eddie is spending a lot of time with boys from the sixth grade, amusing them by annoying other children at their request. The teacher suspects that Eddie is spending time at one of their homes after school as well. She has spoken to Eddie's mother about this, but his mother is aware and does not see any problem. Eddie's teacher reports that neither she, nor any of Eddie's previous teachers, has ever met or spoken to his father.

The only dealings that the nurse has had with Eddie was to administer first aid after a fight. However, she sees Eddie's younger sister quite often, for complaints about headaches and stomachaches. She seems fearful about contact with home, but when the nurse speaks to the child's mother, she always responds to the nurse in a concerned and appropriate manner. When the nurse initially receives the referral about Eddie, she remembers that he appeared to know more information than the other children about alcohol, and equated any intake of alcohol with being drunk. When she spoke to him after class about this, he deflects her questions and says he knows about alcohol from TV. She "left the door open" for him to talk at any future time.

An initial plan of action is developed.

- More information needs to be obtained about Eddie's activities with the group of boys from the sixth grade. Teachers, bus aides, and the boys' parents will be alerted.

- Because Eddie is unwilling to speak to the nurse, teacher, or counselor, the physical education teacher, who gave the most positive report of Eddie's behavior and relationship to him, will be asked to try to work with Eddie as the contact person.
- The principal will set up a conference with both of Eddie's parents, scheduling the meeting in the evening if necessary, to accommodate Eddie's father. Eddie's teacher and the counselor will also be present.
- The team will meet in two days, following these initial actions, to share information and plan for the parent conference.

### Team Meeting #2

It is learned that Eddie has been spending time at the home of a sixth grade boy whose parents are not at home until evening. When the boy's parents are contacted, they are unaware that other children are in their home in their absence. The father calls the teacher back later and reports that the boy has confirmed what was happening. Although the boy says they were just "hanging out and watching movies," the father checks the liquor cabinet and notices some of the bottles are almost empty. The teacher arranges for them to come to school to work together to address the situation, and says she will contact the parents of the other boys as well.

Meanwhile, the physical education teacher has spent some time with Eddie, who has agreed to help him coach the younger children with softball.

Eddie's mother calls the principal and says that her husband will not be able to attend the conference they had agreed upon, and has not responded favorably to the principal's offer to reschedule for his convenience. When the principal calls her back after the team meeting to report the new information about the possibility of Eddie's drinking, she becomes distraught and says she will come in immediately. In the interim, the principal meets with Eddie to confront him with the information.

### Parent Conference

Eddie's mother listens to the account of what may have been happening at the other boy's home. She begins to cry and says she is so worried about Eddie becoming "like his father." When asked to elaborate, she tells the principal that Eddie's father "occasionally has a drinking problem" and many times he does not come home at all. She feels he is a good man, but "sometimes disappoints the children." The principal thanks her for her candor and promises that the information will not be shared with other personnel (with the exception of the counselor and teacher who are present at this meeting) without her permission. The counselor says that there are many ways Eddie's mother can get help for herself and her children. She mentions Alanon as a support group for her to understand what her husband is experiencing and to help her deal with the situation. Eddie and his sister can participate, if they agree, in a support group at school for children who need information about drug and alcohol use, coping skills, and personal growth. If a need for outside counseling is determined, the counselor will speak to her then about suggested referrals.

Eddie's mother is told to use her judgment as to the advisability of sharing this information with her husband at this time. Eddie is brought into the conference and the counselor gently repeats what they had been discussing. He stresses to Eddie that his mother is very concerned about his welfare and has shared some of what is going on at home with them. Eddie looks somewhat puzzled. His mother says, "You know, about Daddy." He appears embarrassed and looks away.

The principal tells Eddie he is requesting that he participate in a special group at school because of his experimentation with alcohol. He says that Eddie needs to understand his feelings about what is going on at home. If Eddie agrees to participate in the group, he can continue to work as a coach for the younger children's softball team. Because the drinking incident did not happen in school, Eddie will not be suspended, but his mother will impose a consequence at home and Eddie will not be allowed to spend time with the older boys in the future. Eddie grudgingly agrees to attend the group, as long as he "didn't have to say anything."

### Outcome

Eddie keeps to his word and does not speak during the first three sessions of the group. Gradually, he begins to become involved in the discussions and completes the sessions as a full participant. Eddie's sister is unwilling to participate in a group setting, so the counselor and teacher use strategies with her to expand her social interactions while giving her information about her father's disease. Eddie's mother never attends any support groups for herself. Eddie continues to help coach various sports and is given an award at the end of the year for outstanding service to others and to the school.

## SUMMARY

Although one in four children live in a chemically dependent family, and they have a much greater chance for becoming addicted to drugs and/or alcohol themselves, schools can provide assistance to help reverse the damaging effects of such a situation. Educators can provide these children with information about the disease and how it affects them and their families. Children can become empowered through counseling and referrals to support groups, and by providing them with alternative adult role models to demonstrate healthy communication and interpersonal relationships.

# CHAPTER 11

# *Death at School*

DEATH IS A reality that our culture seems reluctant to face. The topic of death is often avoided in the educational setting, or acknowledged only by the use of euphemisms. Most people would agree that the discomfort level is high for this disturbing topic. Children and school personnel, although faced with the reality that thousands of school children die each year, seem ill equipped to cope effectively with the aftermath. One out of every seven children experiences the death of a parent before the age of ten (Lord, 1990). Siblings die, pets die, friends die. Furthermore, classmates of children who have lost a parent often become concerned about the possibility of losing their own parents.

The aftermath of a death that affects many children in a given classroom can be overwhelming to the school personnel who deal with them. Children who are grieving find it difficult to concentrate; they may need help in expressing what they are feeling. The adults may feel at a loss as to what to say and how to help. The task of helping children understand death, while most often thought of as a parent's responsibility, also belongs in part to school personnel. Students in their care for a large portion of the day will exhibit signs of grieving that must be addressed.

Sometimes, news of a death will arrive during the school day. The deaths of the Challenger astronauts, which occurred tragically and unexpectedly before the eyes of millions of children, prompted school personnel to respond to the grief, confusion, and fear that children were experiencing.

What seems most difficult in helping children deal effectively with death is the distress many adults feel at the idea of having to address an issue that they themselves have not yet resolved. As a result, many school personnel do harm to children by avoiding the issue altogether; others say and do things that may confuse children or inadvertently increase their hurt (Cunningham and Hare, 1989). Teachers may be unfamiliar with the range of behaviors that children manifest in response

117

to the death of a significant person. They may need clarification as to what is an appropriate duration of grieving. Many teachers mistakenly expect this process to be over in a few weeks (Cunningham and Hare, 1989). Learning the steps of this normal process will assist them in determining if behaviors exist that may require professional help.

## WHAT ARE THE BEHAVIORAL SIGNS OF BEREAVEMENT IN CHILDREN?

Although all children are individuals and will grieve differently, certain behaviors or responses will most often be present in the aftermath of a death.

### Ages Six to Eight

Developmentally, the understanding of the concept of time is limited, which makes the permanence of death difficult to understand. Children see death as something outside of their world, like an "angel of death." Questions about death tend to focus on the biological process of what happens to the body (Ragouzeos, 1987). Teachers should attempt to answer every question even if their response to certain questions is truthfully, "I do not know."

### Ages Nine to Eleven

Developmentally, these children are better able to grasp the inevitability of death. However, they may believe they have caused someone's death by misbehaving or wishing harm to someone. Children at this age may become obsessively fearful about the possible loss of a parent, or may seem to behave indifferently. A facade of joking about death may be adopted by some children who grieve (Ragouzeos).

### Adolescence

Developmentally, the focus is on control. Adolescents can become overwhelmed by their emotions in dealing with death; anger and swift mood swings characterize their grieving. Often, unresolved grief can lead to acting-out and antisocial behaviors (Ragouzeos).

Other behavioral manifestations of grief are:

- reluctance to attend school for fear of another tragedy or loss happening to the child or someone close to him/her
- eating and sleep disturbances
- difficulty concentrating
- acting-out or aggressive behavior (in older children, delinquency and drug/alcohol use)
- anxious, fearful behavior
- preoccupation or discussion of guilt and responsibility for the death
- lack of verbalizations, sometimes resulting in selective mutism, unspoken questions, and reenactments with toys or imaginary play
- regressive behavior, adopting infantile habits and mannerisms
- physical complaints

Should any of these reactions persist for many weeks or acutely interfere with a student's functioning, professional help may be indicated.

## WHAT IS THE SCHOOL'S ROLE WITH THE GRIEVING CHILD?

As previously mentioned, school personnel are often somewhat hesitant about addressing the issue of death with their students. They need to understand their role in the grieving process of the students. Administrators should develop procedures for addressing such situations and provide training for staff so that these procedures may be effectively implemented. Staff members need to feel confident that there are definite roles for them to play both in the initial wake of a death that affects students and in the days and weeks that follow.

In order to help these children most effectively, school personnel should be provided with training to help them understand the grieving process and know how to respond to a child's grief in the educational setting. Because the circumstances of the death will require different responses from staff, training should prepare staff for the death of a student, a staff member, and/or a sibling or parent of a student. These situations will require the activation of a response plan, which will be discussed in the following section. Staff members should be given the following guidelines for discussing death with children.

- The information passed on should be accurate and previously approved for disclosure from the survivors of the deceased. Details about the death should not be graphic, but as complete as possible for the children to understand.
- Teachers should share their own feelings with the class about the loss. They should also open the floor to questions from the class, prefacing with, "I will answer as many questions as I can."
- Children who repeatedly ask the same question indicate a need for reassurance and not a rejection of the helpfulness of your previous answers.
- Children who ask no questions may be having great difficulty verbalizing their feelings. They should not be prompted to talk at this time.
- Some children may say things that sound callous, such as, "He was going to be my partner in the science project. Why didn't he wait until then?" These remarks help children make the death a reality that is integrated into their day-to-day life.
- Children who express that they are sad or frightened must have these feelings validated by the adult. It is a temptation to protect them from these painful feelings, but minimizing genuine feelings is damaging in the long run. "I know how scary this must seem to you" and other such active listening responses enable children to safely express their grief and move through the process in a nonrepressed way.
- Children, like adults, often wish to help the survivors in some way. Taking positive action is a powerful way to deal constructively with grief. Children may wish to make something for the family, or to send a donation to a charity in remembrance of the deceased. The wishes of the family and the judgment of the teacher as to the participation of the class in funeral services should be considered.
- The class may be asked to identify ways they wish to remember the deceased. Stories about the person may be shared so that children can choose special qualities to reflect upon in the coming weeks.
- After discussions such as these, the class should be given a recess or a structured activity for physical play. Children's attention spans are brief; they also need physical relief from emotional stress.
- Children should be helped to understand that although everyone

is feeling very sad now, they will feel better as time passes. They should understand that each person grieves differently, with some taking more time than others, and all showing grief in different ways. In the meantime, they should know that the regular classroom activities will continue, with all of you doing the best you can.

- Children need to know it is not disrespectful to laugh and have fun. Life will go on, but this does not mean that the person is forgotten.
- Counseling personnel may work individually with students who seem to be feeling responsible for the death because of a previous incident or thoughts of unkindness toward the deceased.

### Death of Grandparents, Nonimmediate Family, and Pets

Most children first become aware of the reality of death when a pet they are caring for dies. The loss of a grandparent may be the first encounter for many other children. School personnel should make every effort to listen well to children who tell them of such a loss. Expressing sorrow and asking the children to explain what happened creates an opportunity for them to express themselves in an accepting atmosphere.

Many times, especially with younger children, discussions about the death of a loved one are censored by the family. Children want to ask questions and when they are not encouraged to do so, or when they receive incomplete information, they often use their imaginations to formulate their beliefs about death. Teachers can validate a child's feeling that death is sad and sometimes frightening, even for adults. By disclosing a personal experience of his/her own, a teacher can share the universality of these feelings. The child can also be asked to share some pleasant memories of the loved one or pet.

If the children give permission, their loss can be shared with the rest of the class in an age-appropriate way. A few moments of discussion among the students about losses they have experienced helps the bereaved students feel less isolated.

### Death of a Student, Parent, or Sibling

Administrators and counseling personnel should develop a response plan to guide the staff in dealing with the death of a student or a teacher, and a plan to deal with the death of a parent or sibling of a student. (The suicide of a staff member or student should have a separate and distinct response plan. Please refer to Chapter 14, Children and Suicide.) Provisions might also be discussed for students who have been reported to the police as missing.

### Sample Procedure for the Death of a Student (Nonsuicide)

- The principal contacts the family to obtain as much complete and accurate information as possible. The family's wishes should be honored about what information may be released to the student's classmates and other school personnel. The family should also make the decision as to whether students should attend funeral services, visit the home, etc.
- The staff is notified of the death by a previously established phone chain. Two meetings are called for the start of school. First, the core team will meet to review their action plan; then the faculty and support staff will meet and be provided with the details of the plan (in the event that the death occurs during school hours, the core team should immediately meet to decide the timelines for informing faculty and students before the close of the school day).
- Locations within the school staffed with counseling personnel, either from existing staff or from local mental health agencies, are established for distraught children to visit during the day. Staff are instructed to send children needing assistance to these locations.
- Teachers should be given the opportunity to speak to counseling personnel about their own grief response. Children will be extremely alert to the reactions of their teachers, looking to them for reassurance and modeling.
- The public address system should *not* be used to announce the death.
- The classmates of the student should be the first to be notified by a trusted adult. It is usually helpful for the teacher and the nurse or counselor to work together for this initial discussion. Other teachers will announce what has happened to their classes using age-appropriate information. (Refer to the following section on discussing death with children for guidelines.)
- Teachers and counselors may lead discussions and provide students with the opportunity to ask questions and share

feelings. The students should be asked how they wish to respond to their classmate's family, e.g., by sending a card, visiting, or making a donation.

- The parents of classmates should be notified via a PTA phone chain.
- If a child has died, his/her desk or belongings should not be removed from the room for several days or used by other students in order to help acknowledge the death (Lord, 1990). (A teacher's belongings should be treated in the same way.)
- Close friends of the student should be seen during the day by counseling personnel and their parents alerted as to their responses.
- Statements to the press about the death should be referred to a designated spokesman (e.g., the principal or information officer).
- The core team should meet at the end of the day to review the effectiveness of the plan and to make adjustments accordingly for the following days.

## Sample Procedure for Death of a Staff Member

The same procedures for the death of a student should be followed, with several additions. When a teacher has died, the principal should arrange for someone known to the children, such as a nurse or a counselor, rather than an unknown substitute, to remain with the class throughout the day. This person can be instrumental in helping with the transition of the teacher who will ultimately take over the class. Outside mental health professionals may be needed to assist because in-house counseling personnel may need help coping with their own grief before they can work with the children.

## Death of a Sibling or Parent of a Student

Even if children do not know the parent or sibling of a classmate, such a death may create anxiety about the possibility of a similar loss in their own families. Teachers should use the guidelines above for discussing death with children. Decisions concerning the class' attendance at funeral services or about the kinds of expressions of sympathy sent to the student should be carefully reviewed by the teacher and the core team.

The most important responsibility of the teacher, however, is to make adequate preparation for the return of the surviving student. The class needs to be sensitized to the needs of the returning child. Discussions can be cofacilitated by the teacher and counselor in which children can be helped to decide what to say to the returning student and how to behave. Children should be encouraged to welcome the student back while acknowledging what has happened with an expression of sorrow. Ignoring the student or behaving in an uncomfortable manner can make the returning student feel isolated.

Returning students themselves should be monitored for signs of trouble. They should be treated as before, however, to establish as much normalcy as possible. With the exception of visits to the counselor or speaking about their loss to the teacher, the students should be subject to the same rules and assignments as their classmates.

In addition to monitoring the returning students, the teacher and counselor should ask them what can be done to make them more comfortable and to offer opportunities for them to have time alone and to speak to the counselor when needed.

## SUMMARY

School personnel have little training and few resources in assisting their students to deal with death. By providing such training and developing response plans before a death that affects students occurs, a school climate is established that reduces the confusion and isolation that often happens when such a tragedy occurs. A unified, consistent, and compassionate response based upon sound information about the grieving process will be a comfort to students and staff alike.

# CHAPTER 12

# School Phobia

THERE ARE VARIOUS students who suffer from emotional problems that are centered on the school setting and whose resistance to attending school is often characterized by paralyzing anxiety (Coolidge, 1979). It is estimated that school phobia occurs in three to seventeen of 1000 school children, with percentages varying according to the ages of the children sampled (Kennedy, 1965). Concentration of incidences of school phobia seems to occur at ages five to seven, upon or shortly after entry to school; at age eleven when children make the transition to a middle school; and at age fourteen, when it is often a sign of depression. Although the incidence of school phobia is relatively rare when compared with other types of concerns, a school-phobic child presents a baffling, disruptive, and acute behavior pattern that both school personnel and parents must address immediately.

## WHAT IS SCHOOL PHOBIA?

School phobia, sometimes termed "school refusal," is characterized by a child's reluctance to attend school. It is distinguished from truancy in that the element of anxiety figures greatly in the avoidance of the school setting. The American Psychiatric Association's classification manual (DSM-III-R) distinguishes school refusal as a manifestation of a separation anxiety disorder, while school phobia is a term for a specific fear of the school situation, even when the parent accompanies the child. There are, however, several characteristics that can be used to describe the phenomenon of an anxiety-based reluctance to attend school. These are:

- demonstration of extreme difficulty in attending school, often resulting in extended periods of absence

- acute and/or prolonged emotional upset that may be manifested by temper tantrums
- extreme fearfulness that harm may come to a parent in the child's absence; sadness and misery at the prospect of attending school
- somatic complaints with no organic basis; complaints of illnesses such as nausea and headache in the morning before school and improvement physically later in the day
- remaining at home with the knowledge of their parents; often, parents feel conflicted about seeming to force a child to attend school when he/she is claiming to be ill or is resisting so strongly
- the absence of any other antisocial disorders or dysfunction; many of these children are excellent academic students

## WHAT CAUSES SCHOOL PHOBIA?

School phobia generally can be divided into two main types: acute and chronic. In acute cases, the child is usually experiencing this phobia for the first time. Most often found in children of younger years, the beginnings of the fearful behavior are usually sudden and dramatic, and only occur with school-related activities. In these cases, a precipitating incident is often present such as:

- initial entry or change of school
- death or divorce in a family
- an embarrassing incident in school
- a frightening or demanding teacher
- returning to school following a prolonged illness
- worry about the health of a parent
- fear of other children's bullying or harassment
- parental cues from their own separation anxiety that invite dependency and/or demanding and tyrannical behavior from the child

However, the phobia may arise without a specific incident. In cases of chronic school phobia there is a global onset, and the disorder most often occurs in older children. There may be an existing pattern of previous refusals to attend school over a period of years. Usually, no precipitating incident can be identified.

## THE SCHOOL'S ROLE IN HELPING THESE STUDENTS

As with most childhood disorders, the involvement of the parents in addressing this problem is critical. It is also necessary to make use of counseling and evaluative personnel to determine the severity of the accompanying emotional disturbance. Often, a referral to an outside therapist for the family is indicated in addition to the immediate school intervention plan.

Because of the accompanying emotional upset and degrees of its severity, there are no indisputable methods for successfully dealing with school phobia. There is a general consensus, however, for using some universal strategies to address the problem. These are:

- Immediate rather than gradual return to school is preferable. This may require the parent to accompany the child to school each day and remain with the child for decreasing amounts of time during the school day.
- Consciously reduce the emphasis on the child's physical complaints. Once the child has been medically examined to rule out organic causes, the child can be told that the school nurse will be available if he/she becomes ill during the day at school.
- Sensitize the classroom teacher to the problem and obtain full support in providing positive reinforcement for the child and implementing other behavioral strategies.
- Provide an outlet for the child to express his/her fears and difficulty in attending school by acknowledging and rewarding efforts to overcome these fears.
- Lay out a day-by-day plan with the parents for getting the child to reenter school while anticipating breakdowns in the plan and providing contingencies and alternatives for parents to use.

## HOW IT WORKS—A CASE STUDY: SCHOOL PHOBIA

Lori, a grade one student, has appeared to be enjoying school for the first three months of the year. However, now her mother reports to the teacher that she is beginning to have great difficulty getting Lori to come to school in the morning. Lori is complaining of stomachaches and headaches. At first, Lori's mother allows her to remain at home. When she notices that Lori always seems fully recovered in the evening and then feels ill again the following morning, she suspects something else is wrong. Lori is seen by a physician who reports no organic cause of her distress.

Lori's mother is concerned about the work she is missing. She also reports that the family is becoming extremely affected by Lori's tantrums and screaming when she and her husband try to get her ready for school. Because Lori has not attended school for the entire week, the teacher suggests to the parent that she bring Lori in on the upcoming Monday. This will give the parents time to prepare Lori for the fact that she will be returning to school and that Monday will be the day. In the meantime, the teacher asks for an emergency meeting of the interdisciplinary team to assist her in setting up a plan for helping to address Lori's problem. The teacher promises to call Lori's mother for a conference the following day to review the plan to be started on Monday.

### The Interdisciplinary Meeting

The teacher presents the background information and asks the team for some suggestions in dealing with Lori, both for the immediate days to follow and after. Because no one can be sure how Lori will behave upon her return, alternatives are suggested for many scenarios.

(*1*) If Lori does not return to school on Monday, the principal will call the parents to request that they bring her in. If they refuse or feel they are unable to do so, they will be asked to come in without Lori to meet with the team for assistance.

(*2*) If Lori comes in and does not cause a disturbance, her mother may remain in the hall outside the classroom to reassure her. However, if Lori does not remain in class or refuses to leave her mother's side, the mother will be asked to return home but remain available by phone should staff be unable to calm Lori. If the teacher is then unable to coax Lori into the class, the counselor will take Lori to her office to calm her and allow her to vent, possibly using drawings or play therapy techniques. The counselor will return Lori to the class when she seems ready.

(*3*) If she can not be engaged by the counselor or teacher and continues her emotional outbursts and refusals to enter the class, her mother will be called in to sit with Lori in the class for the remainder of the day.

Lori's parents will be asked to reinforce with Lori the idea of being allowed to call home at regular intervals if she agrees to remain without her mother. She will be permitted to speak to a parent or grandparent once in the morning and again in the afternoon upon her request, but at no other times.

Lori's parents will also be told to advise Lori to ask to see the nurse if she continually complains to them about being ill. The nurse will try to keep to the assigned times for Lori to call home and attempt to involve the counselor in talking to Lori rather than to emphasize her physical complaints.

The teacher will set up a behavior plan with Lori once she returns to school. The teacher will construct a daily checklist that includes various tasks, the first of which may be for Lori to enter the class and return to her seat without crying. Other activities might be to become involved in play with another child, to complete a fun assignment such as an art project, to refrain from asking to call home more than at the assigned times or to go to recess and special classes without crying or refusing. Lori should be made to understand that the purpose of this plan is to help her overcome what is a difficult and scary problem for her. Lori will receive a check for anything she accomplishes, and no check for when she does not. In addition to praising Lori for each task accomplished, parents and teacher will tailor the reward for Lori to receive for each task completed.

The counselor may make recommendations for outside counseling based upon her sessions with Lori.

### The Following Day

The parent conference is held and the plan explained. Those present agree to tell Lori that she will be going back to school on Monday and that they will take her there despite her resistance. Rewards are arranged for Lori if she meets with any success.

### Monday Morning

Lori enters the building screaming and struggling with her mother who is trying to bring her to her classroom. The principal meets them and begins talking to Lori to calm her. Lori continues to scream, saying she does not feel well and she wants to return home. The principal brings Lori into his office, summons the counselor and nurse, and instructs the mother to wait outside. The nurse tells Lori that she has heard she is not feeling well. They have some conversation about Lori's stomachache and then the nurse takes Lori's temperature. In the meantime, the counselor speaks softly to Lori about how difficult it seems to be for Lori to be in school. She tells Lori that her teacher and classmates, especially (and she named two children who had been friends with her) have missed her and are looking forward to her return. Lori stops crying but continues to ask to leave.

The principal tells Lori that she will need to remain in school today, but she can have her mother remain with her just for today. Lori will also be seen by the counselor for a session that day while her mother remains outside the room. At the end of the day, Lori and her mother will sit down with the teacher and go over the behavioral plan for the following days, with rewards designated and times to phone home assigned.

Lori walks to the classroom with her mother. The teacher meets them before they enter and welcomes a sullen Lori. She brings both of them in, introduces the mother, and the children greet them. The teacher immediately introduces the lesson and begins getting the children involved. Lori, although refusing to participate, sits quietly at her desk occasionally glancing back at her mother sitting at the back of the room.

The counseling session is somewhat productive in that Lori talks about her need to be home with her mother and her younger brother. She is angry that no one will honor her wishes or believe that she is sick. Lori's fears are explored to help the counselor understand what stimuli can be adjusted to make Lori more comfortable.

At the end of the day, Lori and her mother sit with the teacher and together they construct Lori's chart. Rewards are established both at school and at home for compliance with the behaviors. These range from special outings for Lori and her parents to Lori's taking care of the hamster in the class. Ultimately, if Lori completes a week without incident (and this is not proposed at this initial meeting) Lori will be allowed to take the hamster home for the weekend.

Lori comes to school the following day and agrees to let her mother leave after recess. Lori phones her in the afternoon at the designated time. She has another session with the counselor. When her mother leaves, Lori cries but remains in the classroom. The teacher praises Lori at her seat for her good behavior in remaining and does not focus on the tears. Gradually, Lori becomes involved in selected class assignments. By the week's end, with continued positive reinforcement and counseling support, Lori can be observed laughing and playing at recess and caring for the hamster.

## SUMMARY

Although school phobia affects a relatively small percentage of students, such incidents are disruptive, damaging to the child, and need immediate and clearcut responses from school personnel and parents. Whether the phobia is of an acute or chronic nature, rapid return to school and the use of positive reinforcement, coupled with an outlet for the child to express his/her fears, can alleviate the symptoms. Some children may be able to overcome these problems through behavioral interventions developed in tandem with school and parents. Others require professional therapy to address severe emotional problems. As with most behavioral interventions, it is important to remember that improved behavior continues to require reinforcement, and temporary reversions to phobic behavior are to be expected and dealt with according to the original plan.

# CHAPTER 13

# Child Abuse and Neglect

THERE HAS BEEN a significant increase in the reporting of child abuse and neglect during the past several years. Despite the fact that some segments of society and cultures believe that parents have the right to discipline their children as they see fit, society in general acknowledges that "carte blanche" for parents sometimes results in physical and emotional harm for the children. Understanding that many parents who abuse their children were abused children themselves, professionals can provide positive interventions that will help the entire family.

All child abuse, however, does not occur in the nuclear family. Consider these statistics from the Child Assault Prevention Program:

- One out of every four girls and one out of every five to seven boys are sexually assaulted at least once before they reach age eighteen.
- Over 80 percent of child assault victims are abused by someone known to them whom they trust. (Preparing children to be wary of a dangerous stranger only partially addresses the problem.)

## RAISING AWARENESS OF CHILD ABUSE

Child abuse prevention programs can help educators, parents, and children to recognize the signs of abuse. These programs are based upon the presumption that caring adults cannot safeguard their children every minute of the day. The National Child Assault Prevention Program (CAP) in Columbus, Ohio recommends that children's abilities should be expanded and strengthened to help them keep safe, rather than to limit their activities. They train children, by use of role play, to assert themselves, to use peer support, and to confide in trusted adults. Children learn to be "safe, strong, and free" by resisting assaults and asserting their personal rights.

Parents Anonymous is a supportive agency that provides information and help for parents who may be at risk for abusing their children.

Together with programs like CAP described previously, the issue of abuse and its frequency can be openly discussed and acknowledged. Information about the presence of alternatives to support parents who wish to break the cycle of abuse has probably averted many instances of physical and emotional abuse of children.

## RECOGNIZING THE SIGNS OF CHILD ABUSE/NEGLECT

Abuse refers to actions such as beatings, excessive corporal punishments, or inappropriate sexual behavior imposed upon the child. Neglect, on the other hand, refers to omissions, such as the failure to provide adequate physical or emotional care. Suspicion of abuse/neglect should be based upon a student's verbal or written complaints, and upon observation of the student's physical condition.

Signs of physical abuse/neglect include:

- unexplained bruises and welts
- unexplained burns (immersion, e.g., socklike, glovelike; cigarette)
- unexplained fractures or lacerations
- consistent hunger, or student consistently comes without lunch
- unattended physical/medical problems

Signs of sexual abuse include:

- difficulty walking or sitting
- torn, stained, or bloody underclothing
- pain, itching in genital area
- poor hygiene, inappropriate dress

School personnel should also be alert for changes in behavior suddenly or over a period of time, such as:

- fearful of contacting parents
- reports injury by parents
- aggression
- withdrawn
- asks for or steals food
- early arrival and late departure from school

- reports no supervision at home
- fatigue, falls asleep
- reluctance to change for gym or participate
- regressive, infantile behavior
- runs away or other delinquent behavior
- developmental lags
- precocious or bizarre sexual behavior

Staff members might also have direct knowledge of a parent/guardian's failure to provide for the student's basic needs and proper level of care.

## REPORTING OF CHILD ABUSE/NEGLECT

Every state has a child protection agency, with which school systems need to develop good working relationships. Administrators must understand child abuse reporting laws and must develop policies and procedures for school personnel to follow when child abuse is suspected.

Generically, child protection laws require any person who *suspects* abuse or neglect to report that suspicion to the child protection agency. Reports can be made anonymously. It is important to stress with the staff that they are not responsible for determining if abuse is indeed taking place. They need only have *reasonable cause to suspect* that the child may be in need of protection because of abuse or neglect. *The protection agency is charged with the task of investigating and determining if an intervention must take place.*

School personnel are protected from reprisals from parents in hold-harmless clauses in the laws that mandate such reporting. The reporting must be done in good faith. Further, adults who *fail* to report a suspected case are subject to fine and/or jail.

Training should also be provided for personnel so that they can recognize the warning signs of abuse and make timely and appropriate reports. Recognizing a child's need for protection is of primary importance to those adults who come in contact with the child. State laws and board policies often require in-service training for professional and support staff to assist them in recognizing the signs of child abuse and neglect. A sample flow chart of reporting procedures, such as the one shown in Figure 7, should be made available to school personnel at the in-service training.

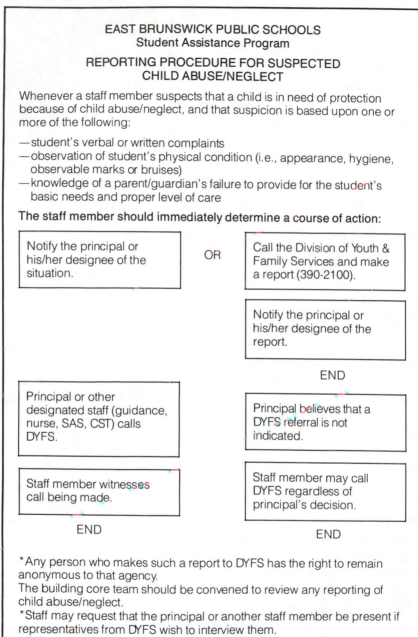

**EAST BRUNSWICK PUBLIC SCHOOLS**
Student Assistance Program

**REPORTING PROCEDURE FOR SUSPECTED
CHILD ABUSE/NEGLECT**

Whenever a staff member suspects that a child is in need of protection because of child abuse/neglect, and that suspicion is based upon one or more of the following:

—student's verbal or written complaints
—observation of student's physical condition (i.e., appearance, hygiene, observable marks or bruises)
—knowledge of a parent/guardian's failure to provide for the student's basic needs and proper level of care

**The staff member should immediately determine a course of action:**

| Notify the principal or his/her designee of the situation. | OR | Call the Division of Youth & Family Services and make a report (390-2100). |
| --- | --- | --- |

Notify the principal or his/her designee of the report.

END

| Principal or other designated staff (guidance, nurse, SAS, CST) calls DYFS. | | Principal believes that a DYFS referral is not indicated. |
| --- | --- | --- |

| Staff member witnesses call being made. | | Staff member may call DYFS regardless of principal's decision. |
| --- | --- | --- |

END                    END

*Any person who makes such a report to DYFS has the right to remain anonymous to that agency.
The building core team should be convened to review any reporting of child abuse/neglect.
*Staff may request that the principal or another staff member be present if representatives from DYFS wish to interview them.
*Failure to report a suspected case may result in a $1,000 fine and up to six months in jail.

*Figure 7. Suspected Child Abuse/Neglect Report Procedures.*

136

# THE SCHOOL'S ROLE IN THE REPORT AND INVESTIGATION OF ABUSE

## *The Report*

Emergency medical procedures should be followed in cases where the child's injuries require prompt action. The person making a report should include:

- names and addresses of the child and his/her parent/guardians
- date of birth of the student
- the nature and possible extent of the child's injuries, abuse, and maltreatment
- any indications of previous injuries or maltreatment
- any other information that is believed helpful with respect to the abuse and identity of the perpetrator

The core team should convene to review any reports of child abuse/neglect.

## *The Investigation*

Employees may be asked to meet with representatives from the child protection agency to provide them with information relevant to the investigation. Such employees may request that the principal or another staff member be present at this interview. Class coverage and a private space should be provided for by the principal. The principal or any other staff member with whom the student is comfortable shall be present during the *student* interview with the child protection agency representative.

The child protection agency may physically remove the child from school or transfer the child from one school to another. Written documentation of such intent should be given to the school by the agency. Student records relevant to the investigation must be released to the child protection agency at its request. Confidential records concerning child abuse cases must be secured and maintained according to law.

The primary counselor (working with the child) will monitor the student and remain in contact with the child protection agency to update the case and ensure continuance of an appropriate educational program for the student.

## HOW IT WORKS—A CASE STUDY: CHILD ABUSE/NEGLECT

Monday morning, the second grade teacher is helping Linda, one of her students, with a zipper that is stuck on her jacket. Because she can not free the zipper, she attempts to take the jacket off over the child's head. As she does this the child winces in pain and begins to cry. The teacher asks the child what is hurting. Linda says that her back hurts because her brother accidentally hit her. The teacher sends another student for the nurse, who comes and escorts Linda to her office. An examination of the child's back reveals several large bruises that are still sore to the touch. When asked by the nurse what caused them, the child says that she had fallen off her bed. The nurse asks what her mother did to take care of the bruises. Linda begins to cry and asks the nurse not to call her mother, because her back does not hurt anymore. The nurse asks Linda what would happen if she did call her mother. Linda just cries and says that her mother "would be mad at me." The nurse asks, "And what would she do?" Linda does not answer.

The nurse tells Linda that she understands she is afraid, but that she would like to help Linda. She calls for the student assistance counselor to join them. The counselor tells Linda that sometimes when children are afraid they do not tell the truth, and that she understands why Linda might not want to tell them what really happened to her back. The counselor says that sometimes children are hurt by their parents, and they are told not to tell anyone or they might get hit again. She also says that sometimes children don't want their parents to get in trouble for what they've done. Linda just listens.

**Counselor:** "Has your mother seen your back?"

**Linda:** "Yes."

**Counselor:** "Did she put anything on it, like ice or some lotion?"

**Linda:** "I think so."

**Counselor:** "Linda, these bruises need to be looked at by a doctor. Who should we call in your house, your mom or your dad?"

**Linda:** "Call my Daddy."

**Counselor:** "Did your mom hit you on the back?"

**Linda:** "She didn't mean it. She said she was sorry and not to tell Daddy."

**Nurse:** "Has mommy ever hurt you before, by accident?"

**Linda:** ''Sometimes, when I'm bad she does.''

**Counselor:** ''Linda, we want to help you and your mommy so that she doesn't hurt you anymore. We are going to call a place that helps children be safe in their homes so they don't have to be afraid of getting hit anymore. We would like you to tell the person from that place what you told us. We will be here with you when she talks with you.''

**Linda:** ''My mommy is going to be mad at me.''

**Counselor:** ''I know you're afraid now. We're also going to call your dad and let him know that some people will be coming to your house to talk to him and your mom about what happened. They will tell your mom that she cannot hit you or hurt you anymore, and they will help her to do that.''

Linda remains with the counselor while the nurse reports to the principal what has taken place. The nurse calls the child protection agency and makes a report, while the principal contacts Linda's father. He reports that he is unaware of any such incident, but that he has been away on weekend business. The principal informs him that Linda will be interviewed at school by the child protection agency before the close of the school day and that the agency worker will then visit Linda's home to interview the parents. The principal suggests that the father be present at home before Linda returns from school in order to meet with the social worker.

The child protection worker spends an hour with Linda, in the presence of the nurse and counselor. Linda reveals that her mother hit her with a shoe on her back. Other incidents have happened, but Linda seems confused about particular details. While Linda is being interviewed, Linda's mother storms into the principal's office demanding to see him. The principal takes her into the office, while she shouts at him that he has no right causing all this trouble, that this is none of his business, and that she will sue him for slander. She says that she was shocked to have her husband call her and accuse her of beating her child.

The principal explains that the school has a responsibility to report any *suspicion* of abuse, and that they do not make such a report lightly. He says that Linda's bruises could not be satisfactorily explained and that she exhibits behavioral signs of abuse. He assures Linda's mother that the school is not accusing her of child abuse, and that she will have the opportunity to explain what is happening to the child protection agency when their worker visits her home later that afternoon. He also tells Linda's mother that Linda's bruises should be looked at by a physician sometime that evening, as they do not appear to be healing well. Linda's mother says she is taking her child out of school immediately. The principal tells her that she needs to go home and wait for Linda and the worker there. He will not release Linda to her without the consent of the child protection worker. The interview is still in progress.

After further discussion, Linda's mother leaves the building. The worker tells the principal that she will accompany Linda to her home. After the parents have been interviewed, she will see that Linda is taken to a physician. Photographs of the bruises will be taken there.

The counselor and nurse hug Linda and tell her she is brave and has done the right thing. Linda leaves with the worker. After dismissal, Linda's teacher, who has been periodically briefed during the day, meets with the core team (principal, nurse, and counselor) to review the situation. It is determined that Linda will be seen by the counselor upon her return to school in the morning, and that the nurse will also see her to check if her bruises have received medical attention. The child protection agency will be called for recommendations on working with Linda. It is understood that the child protection agency will not be able to disclose their findings, but will merely report whether the case will be active or not. They will, however, provide suggestions for assisting Linda at this difficult time.

### The Following Morning

Linda returns to school and is met by the nurse, who examines her back and sees that it has been treated. Linda tells her and the counselor that the worker talked to her parents and that her mother had not scolded her. She did feel that her mother was mad at her, but her father told her that she must tell him right away if anything like that happens again. The counselor and nurse tell Linda that she did the right thing. They encourage her to tell them if she is ever hurt again.

### Outcome

There are no further incidents of abuse reported during the remainder of the year. In grade three, Linda reports that her mother is hitting her again, although no marks are present. The child protection agency is called, and the case is reopened.

## SUMMARY

Often when a young, school-aged child is abused, educators may be the first people to spot the abuse. They must be prepared to identify, respond, and offer appropriate assistance to these children in order to gain protection for them in this crisis situation. This chapter dealt with the school's role in recognizing the signs of abuse and neglect, making appropriate reports, and cooperating with the child protection agency as dictated by the law.

# CHAPTER 14

# Children and Suicide

IT IS RECOGNIZED that the suicide rate for adolescents has tripled in the past twenty years (Wellman, 1984). Much progress has been made at the secondary level to address suicide prevention by providing staff and student training in recognizing signs of risk and accessing help. Policies and procedures have been developed to deal with suicide attempts and the aftermath of a completed suicide. It is rare, however, for an elementary school to give the same kind of attention to suicide prevention.

Although the suicide rate among children younger than fourteen is considerably lower than that of adolescents, approximately 10 percent of all child suicide attempts will succeed (Herring, 1990). Nearly 200 suicides by children younger than fourteen are committed annually (Rosenbaum and Seligman, 1984). Although these figures make the occurrence of childhood suicide seem rare, the incidence of suicidal threats and attempts among children not previously identified as having mental disturbances was reported to be as high as 12 percent (Pfeffer, 1985). Another factor that may skew accurate measures of childhood suicide attempts is the reporting of these attempts as "accidents" by parents or physicians who may not have understood the child's unexpressed intentions.

Because of the difficulty many adults have in accepting the reality of childhood suicidal ideation, many children who are at risk for suicide may go unnoticed. Often, children have difficulty verbalizing their thoughts or feelings. They seldom seek out counselors or adults for help with their suicidal thoughts and often pledge their friends to secrecy (Herring, 1990). Elementary school personnel require special training to understand the risk factors for their young students and how to intervene effectively to prevent such a tragedy.

143

## DEFINING RISK FACTORS OF CHILDHOOD SUICIDE

As children's lives become more complicated, the stress increases, causing emotional overload (Elkind, 1984). Although the presence of one of the following precipitating factors cannot predict suicidal behavior, these factors have been found repeatedly in the children who have attempted suicide.

### Childhood Depression

The growing awareness of childhood depression, a condition that was previously thought not to exist, should prove to be as helpful for child advocacy as the recent increased awareness of child abuse (Hart, 1991). Because the signs and symptoms of childhood depression differ somewhat from adult depression, behaviors may be easily attributed to other causes. In addition to the physical complaints, sleep disturbances, loss of appetite, feelings of hopelessness and lack of control that are usually associated with depression, children may engage in angry acting-out behavior, school phobia, drug and criminal experimentation, and attention-getting behaviors. Suicidal threats and attempts can be a manifestation of this depression.

### Precipitating Events

Although a child may experience one or more of these events, suicidal behavior does not necessarily follow. The importance of the quality and consistency of the support available to a child when faced with these situations makes all the difference in his/her ability to cope or his/her desire for escape through self-destruction. Precipitating events include:

- a suicidal parent, especially a mother
- continued physical violence between parents
- physical abuse/sexual abuse
- chronic illness of a parent or sibling
- divorce or the death of a parent
- difficulty coming to terms with reality of death
- inability to meet impossible, perfectionistic standards
- family crisis in which child is expected to assume responsibilities that are not age-appropriate
- difficulties with peer acceptance

Another situation that can precipitate suicide is a child's inability to meet standards expected of him/her. Children who are identified as gifted and talented at an early age may feel special pressure to achieve, often fighting to attain impossible, perfectionistic standards. Failure to meet these standards may result in extreme tension, manifested in a withdrawal from the social aspect of their lives and an increasing isolation and inability to have fun.

The other side of this same coin involves students who possess a learning disability. Statistics show that 36 percent of the children who have attempted suicide are learning disabled. When compared to the 5 percent of the school population identified as learning disabled, this is an alarming overrepresentation (Pfeffer, 1979).

## WHAT IS THE SCHOOL'S ROLE IN PREVENTING CHILDHOOD SUICIDE?

### *Staff and Parent Training*

It is crucial, especially at the elementary level, to raise the awareness of the reality of childhood suicide. Training for staff and parents on suicide awareness and their roles in its prevention should be provided. Parent sessions should include an overview of the problem, an explanation of the behaviors and precipitating factors that may put a child at risk for suicide, and ways to help the child. Specific school and community resources should be clearly and carefully explained.

Staff training, while including all of the elements of the parent session, should focus on the identification of children at risk for suicide and determination of appropriate responses to such children. For these purposes the school should adopt a standard policy and procedure for dealing with children at risk for suicide. These procedures should also make provisions for dealing with suicide attempts and completed suicides.

### *Developing Suicide Prevention Policy and Procedures*

The core team should be instrumental in developing a response procedure that is workable with the staff, while ensuring the best possible care for the student. The procedure should be composed of the following parts:

(*1*)  What constitutes a risk of suicide for a student?

(*2*)  If risk is determined, what immediate steps are taken by the adult assessing the risk? How does the core team support this process?

(*3*)  What precautions need to be taken to ensure the safety of the child?

(*4*)  When and how are the parents notified? What happens if they cannot be reached?

(*5*)  What are the limits of confidentiality in terms of disclosing information about the child to parents, other staff, and an outside treatment provider?

(*6*)  How are affected others (siblings, friends, etc.) responded to?

### Sample Procedure for Responding to Risk of Suicide

A staff member is concerned about the possibility of a student attempting suicide because of one or more of the following situations:

(*1*)  The student has directly or indirectly expressed thoughts about suicide, either verbally or through writing or drawings.

(*2*)  The staff member notices suspicious marks or cuts on the student's wrists, neck, etc., that may suggest a suicidal gesture.

(*3*)  A third party (peer, family member, adult, etc.) contacts the staff member about his/her concern for a student he/she feels is at risk for suicide.

(*4*)  The staff member learns of a previous suicide attempt of which the school and/or parent is unaware.

(*5*)  The student's behavior reflects that of a person at risk for suicide, such as:
  • sudden and continued change in usual behavior
  • withdrawal from family and friends
  • severe changes in eating and sleeping habits
  • breakdown of family structure due to death, divorce, or parental rejection
  • use of drugs or alcohol or other destructive behaviors
  • giving away cherished possessions

Note: Any of these signs in isolation may be representative of other causes. In combination, they deserve serious consideration.

The staff member, upon noting such signs, shall immediately notify the principal, who will in turn contact appropriate and available school personnel (e.g., guidance counselor, child study team member, student assistance counselor). The staff member will then accompany the student to the designated place of meeting with the appropriate staff member, herein called the primary counselor.

The primary counselor, upon receiving notification of a student at risk for suicide, will perform an initial assessment for lethality (seriousness of intent, ability and means to perform the act, etc.). Throughout this process the student should not be left alone or allowed to leave the room unaccompanied by an adult. The counselor will then contact the parent, regardless of the degree of risk assessed, inform the parent of the situation, and advise him/her of recommended action to be taken.

In cases where the primary counselor has assessed a high or questionable degree of risk, the principal shall assemble the building core team to assist the primary counselor in dealing with the situation. A member of the core team may provide coverage of the student while the primary counselor reports the status of the situation to the remainder of the team. Core team members may help with phone calls, assist the primary counselor in decision making, and respond to other students who may be affected by the situation.

The principal will also insist that the parent come to school, to be apprised of the situation and accompany the student to a catchment area hospital or an equivalent agency or provider for the purposes of a suicide lethality assessment. If the parent cannot be reached or refuses to come to school for the aforementioned purpose, the principal *must not allow the child to return home unescorted*. Several options may be considered by the core team, including transporting the student to the catchment area hospital as per emergency procedures or designating a core team member to remain with the student until the parent can be reached. The principal should report parents who refuse to follow the recommendations of the core team for outside assessment of suicidal risk to the child protection agency for suspicion of negligence.

In cases where the primary counselor assesses no degree of risk, the parents are notified of the situation, the student is returned to class, and the referring staff member is thanked for the referral and instructed to report any other future behaviors that may suggest suicidal risk.

Any suicide or attempted suicide shall be labelled as a "crisis." Professional staff shall refer to the procedures outlined in the district's Crisis Response Plan.

A student's reentry into the school system following a suicide attempt (i.e., any self-inflicted injury that is life-threatening) shall comply with the following guidelines.

A mandatory reentry conference will be provided for a returning student and his/her parents by members of the core team. The following information is to be presented by the family at such time:

- a written report prepared by the treating physician certifying that the student is physically and mentally able to return to school
- a prescription for follow-up care

Students reentering school with proper documentation will be assigned to a core team member, who will provide monitoring and support for the student as long as such services are deemed necessary by the core team. Contact with the student's family will be maintained in order to extend support, encourage parental involvement and report progress. If a parent does not appear at the reentry conference or provide the aforementioned documentation following the student's release from the hospital/treatment facility, he/she will be contacted by the principal. The student may not remain in school without such documentation. Every effort will be made to assist the parent in identifying community resources that provide the appropriate care. Any failure by the parent to comply with reentry procedures will require the school to file a child neglect complaint with the child protection agency.

## THE LETHALITY ASSESSMENT

Counseling personnel—whether child study team, guidance, or student assistance counselors—should understand how to conduct a lethality assessment for children. When conducting a screening to assess the degree of risk for suicide, counselors should determine the following:

- What observable, behavioral signs of risk exist?
- Does the child admit to wanting to kill him/herself?
- If so, does the child have a plan?
- Does the child have the means, or access to the means, to carry out the plan?
- How clearly is the child thinking?
- Is the child impulsive? How much control is he/she exhibiting?
- How hopeless or helpless does the child seem or report to be?

- How often does the child think about suicide? When do these thoughts occur?
- Has the child made any previous threats, gestures, or attempts?
- Has the child told anyone else of these thoughts?

The counselor should use his/her skills to determine how to proceed with these questions, or when to cease questioning once a high degree of risk has been determined.

## HOW IT WORKS—A CASE STUDY: SUICIDE PREVENTION

Michael is a grade four child in the district. During a health class, he mentions to the nurse that his parents are fighting a great deal and that he thinks about running away when this happens. When the nurse speaks to Michael about this after class, he tells her that sometimes he "doesn't want to be alive anymore." The nurse tells Michael that he must feel very sad at those times. She says that she would like him to speak to Mr. Arnet, the student assistance counselor, who might be able to help Michael with how he is feeling. The nurse speaks to his teacher and asks her to see that Michael remains with her in the classroom while the principal and Mr. Arnet are notified.

Mr. Arnet comes to the classroom and accompanies Michael to his office. In the meantime, the principal, after speaking with the nurse, alerts the child study team that Mr. Arnet is conducting a lethality assessment for suicide on a fourth grade student.

Mr. Arnet tells Michael that he is very concerned about him. He says that sometimes other children have said such things to him about wishing to be dead. They say these things when they are feeling angry or sad, and think they might feel better if they were dead. Mr. Arnet asks Michael how he is feeling. Michael tells him that he thinks a great deal about running away but feels it is "dangerous." Other thoughts that had occurred to him involve taking something sharp out of the garbage and cutting himself. Michael also thinks about using a kitchen knife to hurt himself. He mentions thinking about "holding my breath for as long as I can" until he becomes unconscious. When asked what he thinks may happen if he lost consciousness, Michael replies that people would notice and care, but his parents would only notice him for five minutes. Michael also states that if he dies, "wherever I go would be better than here."

Michael's perception of his home situation is one of often getting blamed for things that went wrong. He feels his sister is treated better by his parents and that they care more for her. Michael also states that he feels as if his body is taking over and he will not be able to control himself to stop from doing something self-destructive.

Mr. Arnet asks the nurse to sit with Michael while he reports to the principal. Mr. Arnet meets with the principal and reviews the information from the session, explaining that he has assessed a high degree of risk and asks the principal to contact the parents to come in immediately. The principal calls Michael's mother and asks her to come in to meet with himself and the counselor about Michael. He tells her not to be alarmed, that Michael is safe and has not hurt himself, but that further discussion is best done when she arrives. Meanwhile, Mr. Arnet informs Michael that his mother is going to come in to speak with them about how he is feeling. Michael becomes angry that his mother has been called. Mr. Arnet explains that he does not want Michael to do anything to hurt himself, and since he cannot be with him all the time, his parents need to be told. He adds that perhaps they can all work together to find some ways to help Michael to feel better.

The nurse remains with Michael while Mr. Arnet speaks to Michael's mother and informs her of what has been said. She is somewhat confused and defensive, saying that Michael is very happy and that he would never do anything to hurt himself and that perhaps he is ''saying these things for attention.'' Mr. Arnet explains that even if that is so, it is a serious matter when a child talks so much about wishing to be dead and has thought through various means to hurt himself. Michael's mother eventually agrees to bring Michael to the area hospital for an assessment for risk of suicide. She signs a release of information so Mr. Arnet can contact the hospital and advise them of the situation. The core team meets when Michael and his mother depart to review the situation.

### The Following Day

Results of the assessment, which are discussed by the hospital worker with Mr. Arnet, indicate that Michael is depressed and anxious. Both he and his family appear to be in need of therapy to deal with the dynamics of how they relate to each other. In addition to their pattern of fighting in front of the children, Michael's parents acknowledge that they have higher expectations for him because his sister has been diagnosed with a learning disability. The family enters therapy. They are encouraged to introduce Michael to recreational activities that are noncompetitive in nature and will allow him to relax and relieve some of his stress. The physical education teacher contacts the family with suggestions to meet this need.

Michael continues to visit Mr. Arnet for monitoring and support purposes. Michael's classroom teacher is instrumental in providing opportunities for cooperative learning experiences in which Michael functions as part of a team to complete projects.

## SUMMARY

The incidence of suicide among elementary school age children is increasing. Accurate statistics are difficult to compile because of the occasions when suicides and attempted suicides are reported as accidents. Schools can prepare their staffs to recognize the signs of suicidal risks by providing training and procedural guidelines for effective response.

# CHAPTER 15

# *Children and AIDS*

AIDS (ACQUIRED IMMUNE Deficiency Syndrome) is a fatal disease caused by a virus (Human Immune Deficiency Virus) that attacks the body's immune system. People do not die of AIDS; however, they die of diseases that their body's damaged immune systems cannot combat. It is estimated that by 1995 almost everyone will know someone who has AIDS or who has been determined to be HIV positive. The human immune deficiency virus is spread through sexual intercourse, use of contaminated needles by drug users, and from mother to baby during pregnancy or shortly after birth through breast milk. Since the advent of routine blood testing, the spread of HIV via blood transfusions has been virtually eliminated. HIV is *not* spread through:

- everyday contact in school, at parties, in the work place, in swimming pools
- insect bites
- saliva, sweat, tears, urine, or a bowel movement
- a kiss
- clothes, a telephone, toilet seat, or through glasses or eating utensils used by someone who has AIDS (U.S. Department of Health and Human Services, 1988)

A person can be infected with HIV without showing any symptoms at all. These people are known as HIV positive. The virus is in their systems; however, they frequently appear healthy for many years and unless tested will not even know they are infected.

## WHO IS THE AIDS-ASSOCIATED CHILD?

There are multiple problems associated with AIDS (Acquired Immune Deficiency Syndrome) and schools. By 1991 approximately 3000 children had full-blown AIDS and another 15,000 were HIV positive.

If a pregnant woman is infected with the virus, she has about a 20 – 40 percent chance of giving birth to an infected child (Boland and Czarniecki, 1991). Improvement in treatment is making it possible for some of the infected children to reach the age where they are entering school. However, the probability of an elementary school having a child with full-blown AIDS is still very small.

The fear of AIDS is for many schools, parents, teachers, and children a serious problem. A 1987 Roper Poll found that AIDS was one of the top three fears of American children; kidnapping and nuclear war were ranked one and two. A 1988 public opinion poll found that 37 percent of adult workers would not use tools that had been touched by someone with AIDS (Herold, 1988). In one extreme case a parent wanted the school to cancel future field trips to a beach area because a hypodermic needle had been spotted at the water's edge. She was terrified that her son had been exposed to AIDS because he had gotten his feet wet in the ocean near where the needle was found. Lack of knowledge is the root of the problem. The school faces at least two situations associated with both the need for knowledge and need to reduce fear. First, all children need to know the facts about AIDS appropriate for their age in order to reduce fear. Older elementary children need to know how to protect themselves from the disease. A second problem for the school arises when a child in school is directly associated with someone who has AIDS, such as a parent. Even though it has been firmly established that even close daily contact with someone with AIDS does not lead to infection, the fear of adults and other children can lead to ostracizing the AIDS-associated child.

Finally, the child who has a family member with any fatal disease will face problems that affect his/her adjustment in school. Frequently, AIDS is associated with a dysfunctional lifestyle such as drug addiction and unstable family environment. More and more frequently, drug-addicted HIV-infected mothers are abandoning their well or infected babies to be brought up in foster care or by relatives. Older children who lose a parent to AIDS may also find themselves either a part of the social welfare system or placed with less than enthusiastic relatives. However, not all children who have a family member with AIDS live in dysfunctional homes.

## THE SCHOOL'S ROLE IN HELPING THESE STUDENTS

### Children with AIDS or Who Are HIV Positive

The time for the school district to begin to deal with the issues associated with AIDS is before there are any local situations associated with the disease. First, children with AIDS or those who are HIV positive have a right to go to school. Only in the case of extremely aggressive behavior on the part of the child or conditions where body fluids cannot be controlled is there justification for segregating the child from the regular classroom. Laws, court decisions, and state education guidelines protect the rights of HIV-infected children to attend school. Some of the strategies the school can implement include:

- Establish district policies and procedures concerning both children and employees who are HIV positive, before a case of AIDS is identified and it becomes an emotionally charged issue.
- Establish policies and procedures for routine sanitation and hygiene when handling body fluids; HIV is not the only disease carried in body fluids, hepatitis, influenza, and salmonella are just some of the others. Have standard procedures in place every day in the school to protect all those in the school from disease.
- Notify parents of children with AIDS or who are HIV positive when other children in the class contract contagious diseases such as chickenpox.
- Protect the child's confidentiality. It is not necessary for everyone in the school to know that the child has AIDS. If the condition is generally known throughout the school, it is not necessary for details of health, behavior, or problems to be discussed.
- Treat the child as one would treat any other child in the class; demonstrate by actions that staff are not afraid.

### Teaching about AIDS/HIV

Knowledge about AIDS and HIV should be part of the regular school curriculum in order to reduce the generalized fear of children, and as they mature to assist them in avoiding behaviors that contribute to the risk of contracting the human immune deficiency virus. When a child or staff member in the school is identified as having AIDS, is rumored to have AIDS, or even has a family member with AIDS, an unreasonable panic can result. Trying to educate faculty, children, and parents concerning the facts in such an atmosphere of fear can be extremely difficult. Some of the ways to teach about AIDS/HIV include:

- Include the study of AIDS/HIV in the regular health curriculum. Many schools nationwide use *Here's Looking at*

*You 2000* as their basic health program (Roberts et al., 1986), for which an AIDS supplement is available. Many state departments and agencies also have curriculum material that is appropriate for elementary-age children.

- Special publications such as *AIDS: A Primer for Children* can be used in school and also sent home (Koch, 1988).
- Orient faculty to the policies concerning sanitary procedures and AIDS (and other diseases), and provide training and materials to staff concerning the facts about AIDS and the transmission of AIDS.
- Include information about AIDS, district policies, and childhood fears of the unknown to parents.

### The AIDS-Associated Child

Children who have family members with any fatal disease are under stress. They may not understand what is going on at home, such as why the person has to go to the hospital or why they themselves have to spend time with a relative. Unlike situations where a child who is dealing with a potential death situation receives the sympathy and support of adults, other children, and the parents of other children, the child who has a family member with AIDS is likely to be scorned. In many cases the nature of the family member's illness may not even be a confirmed case of AIDS. Rumor can be as damaging as fact. The teacher in the classroom should treat the child in the same way that he/she would treat another child with an ill family member. It is essential to observe the following practices:

- Maintain the routines and structure in the classroom.
- Maintain high expectations for the child. Don't fall into the trap of thinking, ''What can you expect of Johnny with his family problems?'' You may have to balance your expectations against real events, such as failure to do homework, for a short time, but you should expect it to be a short time.
- Avoid prejudice. How the family member with AIDS acquired the disease should not be the concern of the school or a basis for prejudice toward the child.
- Provide extra reinforcement to show you value the child, such as saying ''I am glad to see you in school today.''
- Let the child talk about the problem. To be a good listener, you

do not need to give advice. Don't assure the child that the family member will definitely get well. Just be supportive and show you care. Let the child know that you recognize his/her pain.

- Do not betray confidences. Things that a child tells you should not be passed on to colleagues. An exception is when the information indicates a danger to the child or another person, as in the case of child abuse. The knowledge that a child has a family member with AIDS is not a danger either to the child or to others.
- Remember that if there is a rumor concerning AIDS in the home, it is not the school's responsibility to confirm or deny it.
- Refuse to tolerate taunting or negative actions toward the child.

## HOW IT WORKS—A CASE STUDY: THE AIDS-ASSOCIATED CHILD

Jennifer is a somewhat quiet child when she enters Mr. Smith's class as a fourth grade student. She is an average student and seems happy in school. She quickly makes friends with three other girls in the class and is accepted by all the other children. Jennifer's aunt comes to school for the first parent conference. She explains that Jennifer's mother is ill and that Jennifer's mother, Jennifer, and Jennifer's four-year-old brother are living with her and her husband. She explains that Jennifer worries about her mother's health. After the winter vacation, Mr. Smith notices a change in Jennifer. She seems withdrawn and she doesn't seem to be close any longer with the other students in the class. One day she bursts into tears. She says she doesn't feel well and wants to go home. She confides to the nurse that she really wants to go home to be with her mother who is now terribly ill. Jennifer's aunt comes for her and confirms that her mother is close to death.

The next day Jennifer's aunt calls to say that the mother has died. The staff feels very sorry for Jennifer. Plans are made to ease her back into the school and to provide extra support when she returns after the funeral. Mr. Smith explains to the class that Jennifer's mother has died and that she will be out for a few days. Suddenly, one of the students asks, "Is it true that she died of AIDS?" Mr. Smith is shocked. While he does not know the nature of the illness, he has never considered AIDS. Another student says she thinks that

Jennifer's mother had cancer. He explains to the class that he doesn't know the cause of Jennifer's mother's death; however, it doesn't make any difference as far as Jennifer is concerned. Jennifer is not sick and she will miss her mother and needs the support of her friends. He gets the class involved in a discussion about losing someone close to you and how it feels. The class suggests ways to help someone who is suffering from grief.

Mr. Smith meets with the principal during lunch. The principal is not concerned about whether or not Jennifer's mother has or has not died of AIDS, but he is concerned about the reaction of staff, parents, and other children if this is the perception. The principal decides to call a core team meeting for after school. When the situation is explained, one of the teachers says that she has also heard from one of her students that the cause of death was AIDS and that the kindergarten teacher has confided that she doesn't want Jennifer's brother in her class the next year. The following action is taken.

The principal places a memo in each teacher's box telling them that, (1) Jennifer's mother has died and that when she returns in a few days, he is sure the staff will be extra supportive, (2) should there be any student or parent with questions concerning the death that they should be referred to him, and (3) there will be a short faculty meeting after school. By noon the rumor was all over the school that Jennifer's mother has died of AIDS.

At the faculty meeting, the principal explains about the rumor. He reiterates that they do not know the cause of death nor will the school attempt to find out the cause. He acknowledges the fear that AIDS provokes. The nurse reviews how AIDS is and is not spread. The district policies on AIDS are reviewed, as is the policy on sanitation. The focus of the meeting is then shifted to strategies for supporting Jennifer when she returns to school.

By noon the next day, three parents have called to ask about the rumor. One parent wants the principal to require that Jennifer be tested for AIDS before she returns to school. Two want their children moved from Mr. Smith's class. The principal explains to the parents who call that the school does not know what was the cause of Jennifer's mother's death. He further explains that there is no reason to think that Jennifer is ill, and that whether her mother died of cancer, AIDS, or some other cause there is no danger to either Jennifer or to other children. He acknowledges their fears but refuses their requests.

The principal also calls a meeting of the PTA board members. The agenda is similar to the one for the faculty. The focus is on controlling fear through knowledge.

When the local newspaper calls, the principal only confirms that a parent of a student has died. He will not give the name of the student. He tells the reporter that the school does not know the cause. When asked how the school would respond if the death was due to AIDS, he says that that would not make any difference to the school, since AIDS would not be a danger in the school setting.

The principal and Mr. Smith attend the service for Jennifer's mother. After the services they tell Jennifer they will be glad when she comes back to school.

The day before Jennifer's return to school, the principal meets with Jennifer's aunt. He explains about the rumor and the action taken. He does not ask for the cause of death. He expresses his hope that Jennifer's return will be a positive experience and that any negative responses will be dealt with directly.

## SUMMARY

AIDS is a fatal disease that infects approximately 3000 children. Another 15,000 are HIV positive and may or may not develop full-blown AIDS. While few children in school have AIDS, children associated with the much larger adult population with AIDS are at risk not from AIDS but from ignorance and prejudice. This chapter dealt with the need for education, establishment of AIDS-related policies, and strategies for dealing with prejudice and misinformation in the school setting.

# CHAPTER 16

# The Physically Unattractive Child

IT WOULD BE nice if people reacted to other people solely in terms of their inner qualities; however, numerous studies confirm that children (Patzer, 1983) and adults (Smith, 1985), including teachers (Richman, 1978), behave differently toward children who do not conform to general conceptions of attractiveness. Physically unattractive children are judged to be less intelligent and less likeable, and receive fewer rewards and less encouragement than attractive children (Smith, 1985). Discrimination against physically unattractive children affects their achievement, peer relationships, and self-esteem throughout their years in school and into adulthood.

## WHO IS THE PHYSICALLY UNATTRACTIVE CHILD?

Children who are viewed as unattractive may be those who:

- have physical abnormalities such as an amputated limb or larger than normal ears
- have a general appearance that varies from the established standard in the school such as the way the child dresses
- have habits that are socially unacceptable such as lack of cleanliness and the presence of unpleasant odor

A child may also have more than one source of unattractiveness. For example, a child with a physical handicap who has been the target of taunts may have low self-esteem and may lack the motivation to maintain adequate grooming. What is unattractive can also vary according to the setting. This is particularly true in terms of dress. For example, school clothing that is typical in one region of the country may appear atypical in another.

## THE SCHOOL'S ROLE IN HELPING THESE STUDENTS

Overt negative behavior toward physically atypical children must not be ignored. Words can be as damaging as physical acts of aggression. Subtle forms of discrimination and prejudice need also to be reviewed and positive action taken. Parents should be involved in meeting the needs of these children. Some of the strategies that can be implemented include:

- Develop awareness of differences among students in the classroom, help children learn what it is like to be handicapped, discuss what it feels like to be the subject of teasing, and develop special activities that allow all children to experience ''being different.''

- Develop awareness among staff concerning their own reactions to physically unattractive children. Whom do they consider unattractive in their class? What are their expectations for these children? How do they respond to these children compared to those considered most attractive?

- Staff should project a clear, consistent message concerning the unacceptability of taunting, other forms of aggression towards, or avoidance of, such children. Discipline should focus on restitution and understanding of the negative nature of the behavior. The child should apologize and demonstrate positive behavior toward the victim.

- Assist the unattractive child in making changes in his/her habits in order to enable him/her to be more accepted. Poor grooming can be approached directly with children. The school nurse and parents can also be helpful in teaching the child grooming skills. Poor grooming can also be a sign of neglect or abuse and may require the intervention of an outside agency.

- Recognize that in some cases differences in dress may be temporary, as in the case of a new student who will soon adjust to the school norm. However, dress which reflects cultural and economic differences will be unlikely to change and should be accepted.

- Student groups, led by an interested and knowledgeable adult, can assist students in learning coping and proactive social skills. Finding out that you are not alone in feeling rejected and sharing with others ways of handling situations can be helpful.

- Establish a plan to assist the rejected child in reentering the mainstream of the classroom. Rewarding positive behavior on the part of the child and of other children in the class toward the child can be very effective.

## HOW IT WORKS—A CASE STUDY: THE UNATTRACTIVE CHILD

John, a second grade student, transferred from another school district in October. He is very withdrawn in class. His clothes frequently appear dirty and he has an unpleasant body odor. The children in the class at first avoid him, and as time goes on a few of the students start to taunt him on the playground, calling him "stinko." John usually does not respond. He sits on the side and does not play with the other children. However, recently he hit one of the boys who taunted him. In class the other children clearly communicate through their expressions and body language that sitting next to John or working with him in cooperative groups is something that they do not like to do. Mrs. Jones, his teacher, has to admit that she dislikes working individually or closely with John. John's parents did not come to back-to-school night and several calls home have not been returned.

### Meeting with John

Mrs. Jones asks John to meet with her for a few minutes at the end of the day. She asks him how he likes the school. He says it is "okay" but that he misses his friend from the other school and he feels funny with the kids in the class. During the meeting Mrs. Jones discovers that John's mother goes to work very early in the morning. His grandmother is there when he is getting ready for school, but he complains that she is always busy with his little brother. John also says that the work seems hard in the class.

### Meeting with the Principal

Mrs. Jones meets with the principal. She feels that John really has two or three problems. First is his physical appearance and odor. Second, the negative reaction of the students in the class. Third, his feelings about and his actual work in class, which confirms that he isn't as prepared for second grade work as many of the other children in class. They determine that a meeting with the mother is a first priority. The principal is able to reach the mother through work and sets up a late afternoon meeting.

### Meeting with the Mother

Mrs. Jones discusses John's adjustment to the school and the problem he is having making friends. She frankly addresses the odor problem and his appearance. The mother confides that John's grandmother is not very well and seems overwhelmed with caring for the children while the mother is at work. John's father has recently left the family and John seems to be becoming more withdrawn at home. The mother has not realized the degree of the cleanliness problem. She decides that she will bathe John at night, and on the weekend prepare his clothes for the week. Mrs. Jones explains some of the steps she will take in class in order to assist John in becoming accepted and in making friends. She suggests that John attend the "Rainbow" group in the school, a group for children who have lost a parent either through divorce, death, or other separation. Finally, John's lack of confidence in his academic ability is discussed. His achievement while not outstanding is not abnormal and he is making progress. It is decided that his needs academically can be met in the class without special remedial help. Mrs. Jones promises to keep the mother informed.

### In the Class

John's appearance does improve immediately and the odor disappears. Mrs. Jones makes a particular effort to reinforce John's achievements in class. She increases her use of cooperative learning groups and sets the groups up so that John will be in a group with children whom she feels will be most sympathetic to John. After a week she plans a lesson about differences among people. The class simulates several situations such as being new to school, being handicapped, and being very shy. The children discuss the situations, share experiences when they felt "different," and suggest ways to include rather than exclude children they perceive as different.

Mrs. Jones also shares the problem and the plan of action with John's other teachers who teach art, music, and physical education. They agree to reinforce Mrs. Jones' efforts. Any taunting of John or any student will not to be tolerated. Mrs. Jones also speaks with the lunchroom aide to be sure that any negative behavior toward John is addressed immediately.

## SUMMARY

Physically unattractive children are responded to in less positive ways than attractive children by teachers, other children, and even parents. Sticks and stones may break bones but words can "break lives." The perception of unattractiveness can be the result of a physical handicap, cultural difference, or developed habits. Adults who work with children must explore their own reactions to, approaches to, and expectations for such children. Positive actions can be taken to assist unattractive children in gaining acceptance. The children can learn to maximize their coping skills. Other children and adults can learn to be more accepting of differences. Classroom and school experiences can be structured to foster acceptance. There should be zero tolerance for the taunting of any child.

# CHAPTER 17

# The Socially Underdeveloped Child

TRADITIONALLY, SCHOOLS HAVE focused their attention on teaching academic subjects. However, in the past three decades the role of the school has been expanded to include such things as drug prevention, sex education, and latch-key programs. These programs have been added in response to the changes in society and the changes in the role of the family in the education of children. James P. Comer astutely points out that when teachers are asked about the major problems in the schools, they list lack of respect and lack of discipline (1988). While impacting on academic learning, these are relationship issues. In the past it was assumed that children would learn to develop positive relationships in the home, and the school's role in this area was that of reinforcement.

Changes in society, such as the increase in single-parent families, increasing incidents of children living in poverty, increased family mobility, increases in children having children, and increased incidents of addiction have also increased the likelihood that there are many children who come to school who have not learned to form positive relationships with adults or with peers. The school and classroom disciplinary code serves as a sound base for what behavior will not be tolerated in school and in the classroom. However, socially underdeveloped children need to learn to establish positive relationships. If they do not learn these needed skills and personal controls, it is unlikely that they will accomplish much in the way of academic learning and will be in conflict with the school environment throughout the mandatory attendance years.

## WHO IS THE SOCIALLY UNDERDEVELOPED CHILD?

The socially underdeveloped child is one who has not learned the interpersonal skills needed to successfully function in the school setting with adults or peers. Typically the child is from a dysfunctional family where he/she is either largely ignored and/or has as role models adults who exhibit negative social skills. In some cases there may be a child who has entered the foster care system and in his/her short life has been placed in many different families. Failure to develop social skills makes it even more likely that this child will have conflicts with foster parents and experience even more changes in family placement. In other cases, poverty and single parenting play a significant role. The parent may need to be away from home for most of the child's waking hours and have little opportunity for interaction with him/her. In many cases it is unclear why a particular child has not developed positive social skills. The failure to develop adequate social skills exists along a continuum. Virtually all children exhibit failure in social skills in certain situations. At the other extreme are children who respond inappropriately to almost all situations. Between the extremes are the majority of children who have many positive skills but deficiencies in some situations.

The following are several characteristics of socially underdeveloped children:

- *Fighting with peers* — since these children have not learned alternative ways to protect their rights, their response is to physically attack if they feel threatened in any way.
- *Withdrawal* — in some cases where these children have found that they are unable to physically protect themselves, their response may be to completely withdraw from interactions with others.
- *Lack of friends* — the child who is unable to respond to peers in ways that are acceptable to other children is often left without friends.
- *Disciplinary referrals* — the child who has not learned control skills acts out in class, violating the rules and receiving the prescribed punishment. His/her response to repeated punishment may be escalation of disruptive behavior or eventually psychological withdrawal from school.
- *Absences from school* — as it becomes clearer to the child that he/she does not fit in the school setting, truancy may become a major problem.

## THE SCHOOL'S ROLE IN HELPING THESE STUDENTS

Socially underdeveloped children can take considerable time away from instructional purposes. In some classrooms there may be a number of such children. The earlier in the grades the problem is addressed, the better. Unless taught positive acceptable behavior, the effect of discipline for negative acts will eventually lose its ability to modify behavior even for short periods of time. Frequently, discipline for negative acts has been the only attempt by the family to modify behavior. No one has made an effort to teach the child how to interact in a positive way with others. In the long run, it will be easier and more effective to teach the socially underdeveloped child social skills than to attempt to modify his/her behavior solely through discipline. Some of the strategies that can be implemented include:

- *Teaching social skills directly and indirectly as part of the curriculum* — health programs such as *Here's Looking at You 2000* have major components concerning social skills. The focus is on developing positive behaviors with peers and adults. Role playing is used to portray various social interactions. Children discuss behavior and their reactions to negative and positive acts. Informally, instruction in social skills can also be worked into the reading class through discussion concerning how the characters interact with each other. Social studies lessons can serve as a base for enhancing social skills.
- *Using instructional strategies to develop social and interpersonal skills* — cooperative learning is ideally suited for this purpose. Children work together in groups on academic tasks, thus creating a reason for productive interaction. In addition, the development of interpersonal skills is explicit in the objectives of cooperative learning. Children discuss not only the outcome of their academic work, but how the group functioned as a whole.
- *Mentoring* — usually socially underdeveloped children have not had a sustained positive relationship with an adult. Mentoring may be a particularly effective means of working with children who have a need to develop interpersonal skills. An adult who focuses all of his/her attention on the child for even a few minutes of the day can have a major influence not only on the child's behavior but also on his/her self-esteem and attitude toward school. Mentoring such children, however, frequently takes great patience and perseverance. Prior experiences with adults may not have been positive, and these children are slow to trust and may continue to "test" the relationship. Nevertheless, once the mentoring is established, the

relationship can influence the academic and social life of the child both in the short and long term.

- *Peer tutoring*—this can also play a role in helping the child develop positive relationships with others. An older tutor may bring added personal stability and also status to the relationship.
- *Discipline*—while not the main strategy for the development of social skills, discipline is however important. Discipline should be consistent and set the boundaries of behavior. When violations occur, the child should have to discuss what positive actions could have been taken in the situation. If the infraction involves another person, the child should apologize and demonstrate the correct behavior.

## HOW IT WORKS—A CASE STUDY: THE SOCIALLY UNDERDEVELOPED CHILD

Jennifer is a first grade student in Mr. Jackson's room. In class she alternates between aggressive behavior and withdrawal. Most of the time she is quiet and seemingly uninvolved in activities; however, she will suddenly strike out at another child if she is accidently bumped or even if someone else uses a crayon she has in front of her. On the playground her behavior is similar. The other children in the class avoid her whenever possible.

### Referral to Student Assistance Team

Mr. Jackson refers Jennifer to the student assistance team. Other teachers confirm that she exhibits inappropriate behavior in their classes. This is particularly true in physical education and art. The school has had little interaction with the home. The parents do not come to school for parent conferences. Telephone contacts have been difficult; usually there is no answer, even fairly late in the evening. On one occasion the teacher did talk to the mother, however, she did not seem interested in how her daughter was doing in school or in her behavior. Jennifer had a number of trips to the nurse in the first three months of school. In the beginning these trips were usually the result of scrapes or bruises she received when fighting on the playground. More recently, Jennifer has complained in class several times about not feeling well and has been sent to the nurse.

The student assistance team decides on the following strategies:

- All of her teachers will emphasize the appropriate behavior that Jennifer should have used whenever she has demonstrated negative behavior.
- Mr. Jackson will develop class activities to teach social skills. He believes these lessons will also be of use to several other students in the class. He will increase the use of cooperative learning.
- The nurse will become the child's mentor. Either at the beginning or end of the day Jennifer will meet with the nurse. Occasionally the nurse will stop into the classroom to see how Jennifer is doing.

## SUMMARY

Socially underdeveloped children need to learn social skills. Discipline may reduce or eliminate negative responses to some situations; however, the negative actions need to be replaced by learned positive responses. There are a number of strategies that teachers can use to develop interpersonal skills in the classroom and in the school setting. These include direct instruction in skills, cooperative learning, mentoring, and discipline that focuses on alternative responses.

# PART FOUR

# *MAKING A DIFFERENCE*

# CHAPTER 18

# *Program Planning, Reporting, and Evaluation*

EDUCATION DOESN'T NEED more programs, what it needs is more programs that work! This is particularly true at the busy elementary school level with the demands of parents, district administrators, board of education members, and the community to teach the basics, score high on the standardized tests, and provide for the artistic, physical, and social development of the children. Schools are expected to meet the demands with limited resources of staff, materials, and time. Added to this in many states and districts are threats of or actual reductions in financial resources. Therefore, any new program or expanded program must demonstrate in concrete terms that it has positive impact on the central purpose of school, namely learning, and that it is cost effective.

Ongoing planning, evaluation, and reporting of the program are essential to successful program development. A comprehensive program for at-risk students has many parts and there are many options both for the individual teacher in the classroom and for the school as a whole. Information is needed on a regular basis to determine what should be added and what needs to be discarded.

Designing the ongoing evaluation is an integral part of planning a successful program. You need to know where you are, what the needs are, and where you are going. Finally you need to know what the signposts are along the way and how you will know when you have arrived. If you have a good written plan for implementing the program, whether it be in a classroom, a school, or a district, you will have the framework for program evaluation and reporting.

## WHAT DO YOU REALLY WANT TO HAPPEN?
## —STATING YOUR OBJECTIVES

A comprehensive program for reducing risks to learning and maximizing learning takes time to implement, time to refine, and time to

175

achieve positive learning results. Therefore, interim process and outcome objectives are necessary, as are final outcome objectives. The final objectives may not be assessed for two, three, or even five years. Interim process and outcome objectives will be assessed annually or more often, based on the plan for implementing the program.

Establishing the timeline for achievement of measurable benchmarks is an important step in planning and implementing a program. While expectations should be set high, they must also be realistic. Too often in our enthusiasm to improve education we oversell to the public and decision makers the potential for quick results. In the case of student assistance programs, there is likely to be an actual increase in the number of children identified as at risk during the second year of the program. Training of staff in identification of at-risk students will lead to this increase in identified students. If the increase is not predicted as part of the program objectives, the increase may be interpreted as an indication that the program is making the situation worse instead of better.

Developing a two- to five-year set of objectives should be part of program planning and the keystone of the evaluation process. Following is a sample set of objectives.

## YEAR ONE

### *Interim Process Objectives*

By June 1993, a more comprehensive student assistance program will have been initiated as evidenced by:

- completion of an initial identification of students in grades K − 8 who demonstrate at-risk behaviors
- completion of training of administrators, teachers, nurses, and nonprofessional staff in identification of at-risk behaviors
- establishment, training, and implementation of the school-level student assistance team
- completion by each teacher of the Classroom Wellness Inventory
- implementation of the revised program for incorporating new students into school
- identification and training of teachers who will serve as student mentors
- completion of training of teachers in grades four to eight in cooperative learning strategies

*Interim Outcome Objective*

By June 1993, 75 percent of the classroom teachers will describe at least one student in each class who is identified as at risk, describe strategies used to reduce risk, and document improvement in achievement and reduction of at-risk behaviors.

## YEAR TWO

*Interim Process Objectives*

By June 1994, the comprehensive student assistance program will have been implemented, as evidenced by:

- completion of training of all teachers in cooperative learning
- hiring of a half-time student assistance specialist for the school
- records of the student assistance team
- implementation of the mentoring program
- implementation of support groups
- records of cooperative work with parents
- assignment of students to classes based on preference for A.M. or P.M. learning in grades one to three, and scheduling of reading and math instruction during the day based on preference
- reduction of within-class grouping for reading instruction, and an increase in flexible grouping and whole-class instruction

*Interim Outcome Objective*

By June 1994, there will be a significant increase in the number of students identified as at-risk and an increase in the number of students served by a comprehensive student assistance program.

## YEAR THREE

*Final Process Objectives*

By June 1995, the comprehensive student assistance program will be fully operational, as evidenced by:

- utilization by teachers of cooperative learning strategies appropriately in instruction
- elimination of homogeneous grouping of students in the classroom, and replacement of these groupings with whole-group instruction and temporary flexible skill groups
- implementation of a plan for reducing at-risk behaviors for students referred to the student assistance team within ten days of referral
- implementation of procedures and strategies for reducing risks for students who are new to the school, non-English speaking, and classified
- completion of training of all teachers in use of learning styles
- implementation of the peer tutoring program
- implementation of the mentoring program

### *Final Outcome Objectives*

By June 1995, students identified and participating in the student assistance program for at least five months will show significant improvement, as evidenced by:

- improved grades
- positive teacher comments on report cards
- a decrease in school-related difficulties such as absences, discipline referrals, and negative progress reports
- an increase in self-esteem

By June 1995, there will be school-wide improvement compared to June 1991, as evidenced by:

- increased student achievement in reading, mathematics, and language arts
- a decrease in discipline referrals
- an increase in attendance rate
- an increase in self-esteem
- a more positive school climate

## DESCRIBING THE PROGRAM—WHAT IT IS, WHAT IT IS NOT

Programs for at-risk students can and do vary tremendously in terms of students to be served, adults to be involved, strategies to be used, and resources to be applied. It is essential in planning, communicating, and evaluating the program to develop a clear concise description of the "who," "what," "when," and "how" of the program. Who is it designed to serve? Will all children in the school be served directly or will only children identified as at risk be involved in the program? What are the main strategies to be used in the program and for whom? When will activities take place, in what order, on what timeline? How will the program be implemented, including the cost? The program description should be written in a manner that is understandable to parents, the board of education, and the community, as well as the professionals in the school.

### Sample Description

The Cedar Elementary School program will use a three-level approach for maximizing the success of all students and for meeting the needs of specific children who are at risk. First, at the school level a student recognition program will be implemented, students will be heterogeneously grouped for all classes, a program for new students will be put in place, the curriculum of social studies will be modified to address prejudice. Second, at the classroom level, homogeneous grouping of students for skill development will be minimized, instruction will take into consideration learning styles, and cooperative learning will be used in combination with other teaching styles. Third, a half-time student assistance specialist and a student assistance team will develop individual plans for addressing the needs of students identified as at risk. The program will be initiated in 1992 and be fully operational and evaluated in the 1994–95 school year.

## DESIGNING THE EVALUATION

The evaluation design does not need to be elaborate. The information necessary for determining the need for the program in the first place and the records kept as the program is implemented serve as the baseline for not only the final evaluation but as the base for decisions during the implementation of the program. The essential part is to plan the evaluation as the program is planned. If the objectives are clear, designing the evaluation is straightforward. Generally the evaluation has two parts — process and outcome.

Process evaluation answers questions concerning the implementation of the program. For example, are the projected number of students to be served actually being served? Do children have different kinds of problems than were originally described? Do the teachers feel that the training they received was adequate for identifying children to be referred to the student assistance team?

Outcome evaluation provides the answers to the "bottom line," i.e., are children better or more successful as a result of the program? For example, do the children served by the program attend school more regularly, have fewer discipline problems, have increased self-esteem, require less remediation, have higher grades?

Sometimes staff feel that conducting an outcome evaluation, particularly one that includes academic achievement, is inappropriate for a program concerned with affect. At least three arguments can be made for the importance of outcome evaluation. First, research has shown that affect is closely related to outcomes such as academic achievement. If students can handle problems more effectively and have increased self-esteem, they will also be able to learn more. If over time this is not the case, it may well be that they have not learned to handle their problems. In other words, the process evaluation may have yielded false information. Second, the bottom line of the school is learning. In an era of ever-tighter resources it is necessary to convince the staff, administration, school board, and public that student assistance programs are not only of value but that they are more valuable than other demands for resources. Third, as children experience more academic success they develop confidence and self-esteem.

If the program has clear process and outcome objectives, then evaluation is straightforward and easy. If the objectives are not clear, the first step is to go back to restate them. Clear objectives are not only essential for evaluation but also for implementation of the program. For each objective, decide what is needed to be known and how the data will be analyzed and recorded. Following are examples of how objectives might be evaluated.

### Teacher Training

A short questionnaire (see Figure 8) may be given at the end of training asking teachers if they think they will be able to use the identification process, and also asking which parts of the training they found were most

```
+--------------------------------------------------------------+
|                    Teacher Questionnaire                      |
|                                          Low  –  High         |
| 1.  Following is a list of some of the areas related to the   |
|     student identification process covered in the training    |
|     session. Please rate each part in terms of how            |
|     adequately you think it was covered:                      |
|     a. peer problems                       1  2  3  4  5      |
|     b. academic problems                   1  2  3  4  5      |
|     c. social skills problems              1  2  3  4  5      |
|     d. psychological problems              1  2  3  4  5      |
|     e. abuse                               1  2  3  4  5      |
|     f. prejudice                           1  2  3  4  5      |
|     g. reporting procedures                1  2  3  4  5      |
| 2.  To what degree do you feel confident that you will        |
|     be able to use the identification process to identify     |
|     high-risk students?                    1  2  3  4  5      |
| 3.  Do you have suggestions for additional training?          |
+--------------------------------------------------------------+
```

*Figure 8. Teacher Questionnaire.*

helpful. Another short questionnaire may be given to the teachers six months later asking similar questions, including whether any at-risk children have been identified and requesting suggestions for further training.

### Student Identification

While the counting of identified students is straightforward in that it is a simple count, it can easily be misinterpreted unless clearly tied to an objective that is understood by all concerned. Typically, the number of students identified as needing student assistance will go up if training and program are effective. If this rise is not predicted in advance, the public and even professionals may interpret the rise as a negative. For example, they may conclude that prior to the program they had never heard of an elementary child who had considered suicide, and now with the program they are being told that three children in their school actually attempted suicide within one year.

Good record keeping is the heart of effective evaluation and reporting. Develop a record sheet for each child referred. Also, develop a format that makes it easy to combine and analyze data. It is extraordinarily difficult to try to go back and collect data after the fact. Decide in advance how the data will be reported. Don't collect a lot of information that can not be analyzed. For example, it is very time-consuming and difficult to extract information from narrative reports in order to summarize information. However, short narrative case studies can be useful and can stand on their own in reports.

### Program Implementation

What happened to children who were identified? What did the core team do? What did the classroom teachers do? What was the parent contact? This kind of information is easier to use if it is recorded on a form rather than if it is reported as an open-ended narrative. The detailed narrative descriptions are important for the individual child's folder and to monitor the interventions planned; however, the form that accumulates data will help in looking at implementation across grade levels, types of problems, and types of children. If not planned in advance it can be extremely time consuming to try to pull all the information wanted from free-form narratives.

### Self-Esteem

There are a number of measures of self-esteem that have been used in clinical and group settings. Those designed for clinical use are usually comprehensive and require special training to administer, score, and interpret data. Some of the group-administered assessments were designed for research purposes and include questions concerning family practices, sexual orientation, and other items that may be resented by the children and their parents.

Psychological Testing Service publishes the *School Attitude Measure* (SAM). This assessment measure is easy to use, focuses on factors related to the child in school, has national norms, and can be used to identify individual students as well as groups of students who may have particular needs. It can be used to assess the overall climate of the school. Finally it can be used as a pre-post measure for groups and individuals.

One way of using the instrument is to administer it as a pretest to all students. Another is to administer it to a sample of students. The instrument can also be used with students who are referred for assistance. While the instrument does not include controversial items, it is a good idea to notify parents and orient staff concerning the instrument and how the data will and will not be used. Parents may be concerned that results may find their way into the child's permanent record, and teachers may be concerned that if their students score low on a subtest such as "motivation toward learning" that the data will be used to evaluate their performance. Following is a description of the factors measured by the SAM:

Motivation for schooling

- willingness to participate in school
- school related to future needs
- importance of school compared to other activities
- how significant others view the importance of school

Academic self-concept – performance-based

- perception of ability to do school tasks
- feelings of importance as a member of the class
- reactions to poor performance
- confidence in ability to perform academically

Academic self-concept – reference-based

- perception of school performance compared to the expectations of others
- student's own expectations about school performance
- willingness to discuss performance with significant others
- comparison of current performance with other appropriate groups

Also measured is the student's sense of control over performance, i.e., the student's feeling about whether he/she is responsible for achievement or whether outcomes are the result of luck, fate, or other outside factors (adapted from *School Attitude Measure – A Comprehensive Assessment Program*, 1989).

### Student Behavior

Some of the ways student behavior can be documented include the number of negative and positive comments on report cards, discipline referral, and attendance records. If this information is recorded for the marking period prior to referral, at the time of referral it can then be used to monitor progress and can be compared to marking period data six months or a year after referral. School-wide data can also be used to evaluate impact on the entire school.

### Student Achievement

Some of the ways student achievement can be documented include changes in grades, teacher ratings, test scores, portfolios, and participation in class. A note of caution concerning standardized test results—if a child has had a serious problem that has affected his/her learning in school over a long period of time, the program may help this child to deal with the problem; however, it will take time to remediate skills missed, and for those results to be reflected in standardized test scores.

## DOES IT WORK?—ANALYZING THE DATA

Analyzing the data should be easy and interesting. It is important to know what is working and what needs to be changed or improved. In evaluating a student assistance program, there are many factors, including different student problems, various strategies for improving school and classroom climate and for addressing individual student problems, varying lengths of time in programs, and different combinations of staff involved in strategies.

It is important that multiple indicators be analyzed in order to get the fullest picture of what is happening (process) and the outcomes that are achieved. However, while it is important to get various types of information, it is not necessary to analyze all the data potentially available. There is some information that must be kept concerning each child identified, i.e., what strategies have been used to address problems and what have been the results of interventions. However, in some cases samples can be used for program evaluation rather than data for all students. For example, there may be standardized assessment scores, grades, and attendance records for all the children in the school, a sample of students in the school and track changes in their performance over time can be selected. The advantage to using a sample for analysis is that in the same amount of time information of different types can be analyzed. There will be a clearer picture of what is happening in the program if changes in attendance, behavior in class, attitude toward school, and achievement in class are known, for example, than if only the analysis of test scores from all 400 students in your school is available for study.

There is no magic number for sample size, usually twenty to twenty-five can be considered a large sample. In some situations there may not be anywhere near twenty cases to study; nevertheless, this data can still be analyzed. Figure 9 shows an example of a sampling plan that might be used at the elementary level.

Some of the above data will be in the form of counts (i.e., numbers of children referred or the number of positive and negative comments on report cards), other data will be in the form of ratings (i.e., teacher rating of training), and some will be in the form of scores (i.e., the attitude test scores). Organizing the data into a chart or graph can help the analyst visualize what is happening in the program and also help communicate the results.

If there is access to a computer, there are a number of easy-to-use programs, such as *Harvard Graphics*, which can make presentation of data simple to produce. Figures 10–16 show several examples of how student assistance data might be organized for reporting and analysis.

Once the data is organized, it must be interpreted. What are the data saying about the program services and the children served? The data

---

**Sampling Plan**

| Data | Size of Sample |
|---|---|
| Program Implementation: | |
| Teacher rating of training | All 20 teachers |
| Ratings of accuracy of referrals | 15 forms |
| Core team reports | 15 reports |
| | |
| Identified At-Risk Students: | |
| Report card comments for the mark- | |
| ing period before identification | 20 primary children |
| and after six months | 20 grade 4–8 children |
| Grades | Same as above |
| Attendance | Same as above |
| Student attitudes data | Same as above |
| | |
| All Students: | |
| Student attitude data school-wide at | |
| the beginning of program and the | |
| same students at the end of each | |
| year. | 20 students each grade |
| Number of disciplinary referrals prior | |
| to program and each year | Same as above |

*Figure 9. Evaluation Sampling Plan.*

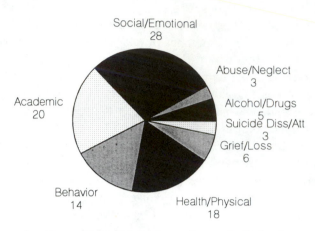

*Figure 10. At-Risk Students — Reason for Referral.*

| Activities | Numbers |
|---|---|
| Total # Referred | 43 |
| Individual Sessions | 248 |
| Group Sessions | 22 |
| Individual Class Plans | 145 |
| Family Sessions | 39 |
| Class Observations | 270 |
| Staff Consultations | 34 |
| Agency Referrals | 23 |
| Core Team Meetings | 39 |
| Crisis Interventions | 4 |
| Teaching Strategies | 62 |
| Peer Tutoring | 15 |
| Mentor Program | 24 |

*Figure 11. Student Assistance Activities — Identified At-Risk Students.*

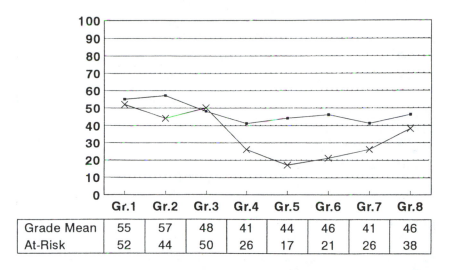

| | Gr.1 | Gr.2 | Gr.3 | Gr.4 | Gr.5 | Gr.6 | Gr.7 | Gr.8 |
|---|---|---|---|---|---|---|---|---|
| Grade Mean | 55 | 57 | 48 | 41 | 44 | 46 | 41 | 46 |
| At-Risk | 52 | 44 | 50 | 26 | 17 | 21 | 26 | 38 |

**─■ Grade Mean ─✕ At-Risk**

NCE Mean Scores

*Figure 12. School Attitude Measure — All Students Compared to At-Risk.*

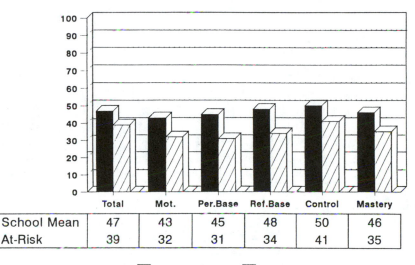

| | Total | Mot. | Per.Base | Ref.Base | Control | Mastery |
|---|---|---|---|---|---|---|
| School Mean | 47 | 43 | 45 | 48 | 50 | 46 |
| At-Risk | 39 | 32 | 31 | 34 | 41 | 35 |

**■ School Mean ▨ At-Risk**

Total Score and Sub-Test Scores

*Figure 13. School Attitude Measure 1991 — All Students Compared to At-Risk.*

187

| Reason for Referral | Year 1 | Year 2 |
|---|---|---|
| Alcohol/Other Drugs | 2 | 4 |
| Suicide Discussed | 2 | 3 |
| Suicide Attempt | 1 | 1 |
| Child Abuse/Neglect | 3 | 6 |
| Social/Peer Problems | 15 | 14 |
| Academic Problems | 20 | 18 |
| Child of Alcoholic | 3 | 9 |
| Grief/Loss | 6 | 5 |
| Emotional | 12 | 11 |
| Eating Disorder | 1 | 2 |
| Behavior | 14 | 12 |
| Physical/Health | 18 | 22 |
| Total | 97 | 107 |

Major reason for referral.

*Figure 14. Reasons for Referral — Students at Risk.*

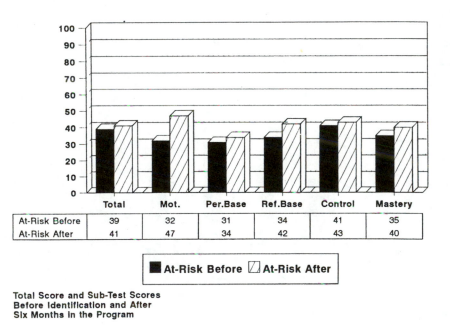

| | Total | Mot. | Per.Base | Ref.Base | Control | Mastery |
|---|---|---|---|---|---|---|
| At-Risk Before | 39 | 32 | 31 | 34 | 41 | 35 |
| At-Risk After | 41 | 47 | 34 | 42 | 43 | 40 |

■ At-Risk Before ◫ At-Risk After

**Total Score and Sub-Test Scores
Before Identification and After
Six Months in the Program**

*Figure 15. School Attitude Measure.*

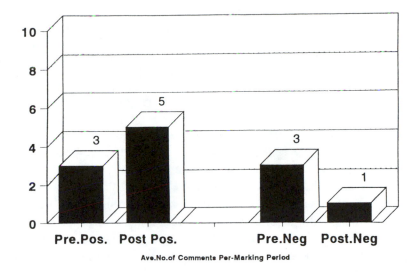

Ave.No.of Comments Per-Marking Period

Aver. no. positive and negative report
card comments before identification and
after a minimum of six months in program

***Figure 16.*** *Report Card Comments.*

presented above on the chart showing pre- and post-report card comments, might be reported as follows:

> Each marking period, teachers communicate with parents by issuing
> grades and writing positive and negative comments on report cards
> related to the child's performance in class. These comments may be
> specific to a subject such as "John needs to be more careful in doing
> computation in math." or "Sue has really improved in reading this
> marking period." Comments may also refer to overall behavior in school,
> such as, "Joe needs to complete homework every day."
>
> When a child is identified as at-risk the number of positive and negative
> comments on his/her report card for the previous marking period are
> recorded on the referral form. The "Report Card Comments" chart
> shows the average number of positive and negative comments for all
> children identified at least six months before the end of school and the
> average number of positive and negative comments for those same
> children during the last marking period of the school year.
>
> The chart clearly shows an increase in positive comments and a decrease
> in negative comments. The results are reflective of more positive results
> in class for at-risk students. At-risk children and their parents are also
> receiving more positive reinforcement. It may be that teachers have

become more aware of a referred child's needs, their expectations for the child may have been heightened, and these factors have affected their perception of the child's behavior. However, sensitivity to and high expectations for children are directly related to the success of children in school. Combined with the other indicators of success such as increased grades and attendance, the positive change in report card comments can be interpreted as supporting the value of the program for at-risk children.

In some cases it is necessary or interesting to go beyond just a reasoned review and interpretation of the data. Apparent differences in figures such as pre-post measures may not be statistically different. There are simple statistical programs available for PC computers that make analysis of data easy and do not require a background in statistics. Since most of the data generated from student assistance programs is fairly subjective, e.g., the number of teacher comments on report cards, a nonparametric test such as the Wilcoxon Matched Pairs test or the Mann Whitney U can be used to test if the results from pre-post data or from two different groups are statistically different. Scaled scores or the NCE's (National Curve Equivalent scores) from standardized tests, such as the *Student Attitude Measure*, can be analyzed using the Parametric T Test.

## REPORTING THE RESULTS OF STUDENT ASSISTANCE PROGRAMS

There are several audiences for reports concerning the student assistance program. The first audience includes those who are responsible for the development and implementation of the program. For this group the report needs to pull the gathered data together and interpret the data in a manner that will guide the future direction of the program. The second audience includes those who have been involved in implementing the program, i.e., the teachers in the classrooms. The third audience includes those who provide resources and support for the program, i.e., central district office staff, board of education members, and grant agencies (such as programs using federal Chapter 2 funds available in all districts). The fourth group consists of parents and taxpayers in the community. Finally, it is valuable to share the results of programs with the profession.

Not only are there various audiences for program reports, there are different interests within the groups. Some people want to see cold hard statistics, while others are interested in getting a "feel" for the program. In order to meet the needs of various audiences and individual interests and at the same time avoid preparing multiple reports, a report with several sections can be prepared. Such a report need not be very long (long reports will be of little interest to any audience), but it should be all-inclusive. For example, the within-school audience knows what the core team is and how it operates; however, the grant agency or board of education may not know or remember. Therefore, the report needs to include descriptions of the "who, what, when, where, and why" of the program. Figure 17 shows a sample report outline with excerpts from reports.

Frequently, in addition to the written report, there are opportunities to make oral reports to groups. In general the same areas need to be covered as in the written report; however, there are ways of making the report more "real" when it is done as a presentation. Overheads can be used to provide structure to the report and to present data visually.

---

1. The need for student assistance programs
2. Description of the program in _____ Elementary School or _____ Middle School
   a. School-wide program
   b. Programs for identified at-risk students
3. Report on activities during the year school-wide
   a. Teacher training, e.g., identification, cooperative learning
   b. Changes in school programs, e.g., elimination of tracking
   c. Changes in policies, e.g., discipline procedures
   d. Changes in teaching strategies, e.g., cooperative learning
   e. Formation and operation of a core team
   f. Development of the crisis plan
   g. Curriculum change, e.g., adoption of *Here's Looking at You 2000*
4. Report on identified at-risk students
   a. Narrative concerning reasons for referral
   b. Chart showing number and reasons for referral in January and for the full year
   c. Chart showing intervention activities for identified children
   d. Two to three case studies (altered to protect the identity of the child)
5. Outcome report (this may be after two or three years) and conclusion
   a. School-wide (increases in achievement, identification, attendance, attitude toward self and school and decreases in negative behaviors)
   b. At-risk students (increases in achievement, attendance, attitude toward self, peers, school and decreases in negative behaviors)

---

*Figure 17. Outline for At-Risk Program Evaluation Report.*

It is important to give the audience a feel for the program. One way to do this is to stage a core team meeting, in which two to three students are discussed. This is another way of presenting case studies. The role of the team becomes apparent, the types of student problems become clear, and the strategies used with at-risk students can be seen. Videotaped segments can also be used to illustrate classroom activities or intervention strategies.

## SUMMARY

This chapter dealt with the importance of planning, reporting, and evaluating the results of student assistance programs both as a means of improving the program and as a means for gaining support for continuation of programs. Detailed approaches were presented for establishing and monitoring a three- to five-year plan, recording and presenting data and finally interpreting and drawing conclusions concerning the program.

# Resource Agencies

THE FOLLOWING AGENCIES provide a wide variety of publications, services and information concerning the risks to learning covered in this book. Many of these agencies can assist schools to contact local services available in the immediate area of the school.

## ALCOHOL AND DRUGS

*Al-Anon Family Groups*, Box 182, Madison Square Station, New York, NY 10159-0182. (212) 683-1771.

*Alcohol, Drug Abuse and Mental Health Administration (ADAMHA)*, 5600 Fishers Lane, Rockville, MD 20857.

*Alcoholics Anonymous*, P.O. Box 459, Grand Central Station, New York, NY 10163. (212) 686-1100.

*Educational Services District # 121*, ''Here's Looking at You, 2000,'' Seattle, WA.

*Families Anonymous*, 14167 Victory, #1, Van Nuys, CA 91411. (818) 989-7841.

*Mothers Against Drunk Driving (MADD)*, 669 Airport Freeway, Suite 310, Hurst, TX 76053. (817) 268-6232.

*Narcotics Education Inc.*, 6830 Laurel St., NW, Washington, DC 20012. (800) 548-8700.

*National Association for Children of Alcoholics*, 31706 Coast Highway, Suite 201, South Laguna, CA 92677. (714) 499-3889.

*National Cocaine Hotline*, (800)-COCAINE.

*National Council on Alcoholism*, 12 West 21st St., 7th Floor, New York, NY 10010. (212) 206-6770.

*National Federation of Parents for Drug Free Youth*, 1820 Franwell Ave., Suite 16, Silver Springs, MD 20902. (301) 649-7100.

*National Institute of Alcohol Abuse and Alcoholism (NIAAA)*, P.O. Box 2345, Rockville, MD 20852. (301) 468-2600 (US Clearinghouse).

*National Institute on Drug Abuse (NIDA)*, Room 10-A-43, 5600 Fisher Lane, Rockville, MD 20852. (301) 443-6500 (US Clearinghouse).

*National PTA, Alcohol Education Publications*, 700 North Rush St., Chicago, IL 60611. (312) 787-0977.

*Parent Resources Institute for Drug Education (PRIDE)* and *Student Resource Institute for Drug Education (STRIDE)*, 100 Edgewood Ave., Suite 1216, Atlanta, GA 30303. (800) 241-9726.

*Target*, National Federation of State High School Associations, 11724 Plaza Circle, P.O. Box 20626, Kansas City, MO 64195. (816) 464-5400.

*Toughlove*, P.O. Box 1069, Doylestown, PA 18901. (215) 348-7090.

## SUICIDE PREVENTION

*National Education Association*, Human and Civil Rights, 1201 16th St., NW, Washington, DC 20036. (202) 833-4000.

*National Institute of Mental Health*, 1021 Prince St., Alexandria, VA 22314.

*Youth Suicide National Center*, 1825 Eye St., NW, Suite 400, Washington, DC 20006. (202) 429-0190.

## CHILD ABUSE

*American Federation of Teachers, AFL-CIO*, 555 New Jersey Ave., NW, Washington, DC 20001. (202) 879-4847.

*Child Assault Prevention Program*, P.O. Box 02084, Columbus, OH 43202. (614) 291-2540.

*National Center on Child Abuse and Neglect*, Children's Bureau, Administration for Children, Youth and Families, US Department of Health and Human Services, P.O. Box 1182, Washington, DC 20013. (202) 245-2840.

*The National Center for Missing and Exploited Children*, 1835 K. St., NW, Suite 700, Washington, DC 20006. (202) 634-3821.

*National Clearinghouse on Child Abuse and Neglect Information*, (301) 251-5157.

*National Council on Child Abuse and Family Violence*, Washington Square, 1050 Conn. Ave., NW, Washington, DC 20036. (202) 429-6695.

*National Education Association*, 1201 16th St., NW, Washington, DC 20036. (202) 833-4000.

*National PTA*, 700 Rush St., Chicago, IL 60611. (312) 787-0977.

*National Runaway Switchboard*, 1-800-621-4000.

*Runaway Hotline*, 1-800-231-6946.

## AIDS

*AIDS Action Council/Federation of AIDS Related Organizations*, 729 8th St., SE, #200, Washington, DC 20003. (202) 547-3101.

*AIDS Education Fund*, 2335 18th St., NW, Washington, DC 20009. (202) 332-5939.

*American Academy of Pediatrics, Office of Government Liaison*, 1331 Pennsylvania Ave., NW, Suite 721 North, Washington, DC 20004. (202) 662-7460.

*American Council of Life Insurance, Health Insurance Association of America*, "Teens and AIDS: Playing it Safe," Department 190, ACLI/HIAA, 1001 Pennsylvania Ave., NW, Washington, DC 20004-2599.

*American Foundation for AIDS Research*, 9601 Wilshire Blvd., Mezzanine, Los Angeles, CA 90210. (213) 273-5547.

*Centers for Disease Control*, 1600 Clifton Rd., Bldg. 6, Room 277, Atlanta, GA 30333. (404) 329-3472.

*Lambda Legal Defense and Education Fund*, 132 W. 43rd St., New York, NY 10036. (212) 944-9488.

*National Coalition of Gay and Sexually Transmitted Disease Services*, P.O. Box 239, Milwaukee, WI 53201. (414) 277-7671.

*National Education Association*, 1201 16th St., NW, Washington, DC 20036. (202) 833-4000.

Adams, R. S. and B. J. Biddle. 1970. *Realities of Teaching: Explorations with Video Tape.* New York: Holt, Rinehart and Winston.

American Association of School Administrators. 1990. *Healthy Kids for the Year 2000: An Action Plan for Schools.* Arlington, Virginia.

American Psychiatric Association. 1987. *Diagnostic and Statistical Manual of Mental Disorders (3rd edition, revised).* Washington, DC.

Birman, B. F., M. E. Orland, R. K. Jung, R. J. Anson, G. N. Garcia, M. T. Moore, J. E. Funkhouser, D. R. Morrison, B. J. Turnbull, and E. R. Reisner. 1987. *The Current Operation of Chapter I Program.* Washington, DC: Office of Educational Research and Improvement, US Department of Education.

Black, C. 1981. *It Will Never Happen to Me.* Newport Beach, CA: ACT Publishing.

Boehnlein, M. 1987. "Reading Intervention for High Risk First Graders," *Educational Leadership*, 44(6):32−37.

Boland, Mary G. and L. Czarniecki. 1991. "Starting Life with HIV," *RN*, January.

Braddock, J. H., II and J. M. McPartland. 1990. "Alternatives to Tracking," *Educational Leadership*, 47(7):76−79.

Brodinsky, B. and K. Keough. 1989. *Students At Risk: Problems and Solutions.* Arlington, Virginia: American Association of School Administrators.

Brophy J. 1983. "Classroom Organization and Management," *The Elementary School Journal*, 83(2):265−286.

Brophy, J. E. and T. L. Good. 1985. "Teacher Behaviors and Student Achievement," in *Handbook of Research on Teaching (3rd edition)*, Witlock, ed., New York: McMillan Publishing Co.

Bruce, M. H. 1976. "Establishing Pre-Instructional Set," in *Skill Building Series: Intern Teaching Program,* Miller, ed., Temple University.

Carter, L. F. 1984. "The Sustaining Effects Study of Compensatory and Elementary Education," *Educational Researcher*, 13(7):4−13.

Cohn, J. 1987. "The Grieving Student," *Instructor* (Jan.):76−79.

Comer, J. P. 1988. "Teaching Social Skills to At-Risk Children," *Education Week* (November 30).

Coolidge, J. C. 1979. "School Phobia," in *Basic Handbook of Child Psychiatry,* J. D. Noshptiz, ed., New York: Basic Books.

Cummings, C. 1983. *Managing to Teach.* Edmonds, Washington: Teaching, Inc.

Cunningham, B. and J. Hare. 1989. "Essential Elements of a Teacher In-Service Program on Child Bereavement," *Elementary School Guidance and Counseling,* 23:175−181.

Dean, L. C. 1989. "COAs: The School's Response," *Student Assistance Journal* (May/June):19−23.

DeFore, D. E., G. S. Pinnell, C. A. Lyons, and P. Young. 1987. *Ohio's Reading Recovery Program.* Columbus, Ohio: Ohio State University.

Deshler, D. D., J. B. Schumaker, G. R. Alley, M. M. Warner, and F. L. Clark. 1982. "Learning Disabilities in Adolescent and Young Adult Populations: Research Implications," *Focus on Exceptional Children,* 15:1−12.

Dunn, R. and K. Dunn. 1978. *Teaching Students Through Their Individual Learning Styles: A Practical Approach.* Reston, VA: Reston Publishing Co.

Educational Research Service. 1990. *What We Know About: Cooperative Learning.* Arlington, Virginia.

Elkind, D. 1984. *The Hurried Child.* Reading, MA: Addison-Wesley.

Epstein, J. L. 1987. "Parent Involvement: What Research Says to Administrators," *Education and Urban Society* (February):119−136.

Gilmartin, B. G. 1987. "Peer Group Antecedents of Severe Love Shyness in Males," *Journal of Personality,* 55:467−489.

Glass, R. S. 1991. "Opening Windows for Teenagers: How Mentors Can Help," *American Education,* 48(Spring):21−26.

Good, T. L. 1982. "How Teachers' Expectations Affect Results," *American Education,* 18(10):25−32.

Good, T. L. and J. E. Brophy. 1984. *Looking Into Classrooms (3rd edition).* New York: Harper and Row.

Gottfridson, G. D. From paper presented at the Annual Convention of the American Educational Research Association, New Orleans, April, 1988.

Hawley, W. and S. Rosenbroltz, with H. Goodstein and T. Hasselbring. 1984. "Good Schools: What Research Says about Improving Student Achievement," *Peabody Journal of Education,* 61(4).

Herold, D. 1988. "When Afraid Comes to Work," *Health News.* Trenton, NJ: St. Francis Medical Center, Trenton, NJ, Autumn.

Herring, R. 1990. "Suicide in the Middle School: Who Said Kids Will Not?" *Elementary School Guidance and Counseling,* 25:129−137.

Hodghenson, H., Director of the Center for Demographic Policy, Washington DC. Remarks from American Association of School Administrators−12th Annual Educational Policy Conference, Washington, DC, 1990.

Hoover, J. and R. J. Hazler. 1991. "Bullies and Victims," *Elementary School Guidance and Counseling*, 25:212−218.

Hunter, M. 1985. *Motivation Theory for Teachers*. El Segundo, California: TIP Publications.

Hunter, M. 1986. *Retention Theory for Teachers*. El Segundo, California: TIP Publications.

Jaynes, J. H. and R. J. Wlodowski. 1990. *Eager to Learn: Helping Children to Become Motivated and Love Learning*. San Francisco: Jossey-Bass Publishers.

Jenkins, J. R. and L. M. Jenkins. 1987. "Making Peer Tutoring Work," *Educational Leadership*, 44(6):64−68.

Johnson, D., R. Johnson, E, Holubec, and P. Roy. 1984. *Circles of Learning*. Alexandria, Virginia: Association of Supervision and Curriculum Development.

Kaeser, S. C. 1985. "Student Participation in Ohio Schools: Attendance and Dropout Date for Ohio Public Schools, 1983−84 School Year," Cleveland, OH: Citizens' Council for Ohio Schools.

Karweit, N. L. 1989. "Preschool Programs for Students at Risk of School Failure," in *Effective Programs for Students at Risk*, R. E. Slavin, N. L. Karweit, and N. A. Madden, eds., Boston: Allyn and Bacon.

Kennedy, W. A. 1965. "School Phobia: Rapid Treatment of Fifty Cases," *Journal of Abnormal Psychology*, 70:285−289.

Kerman, S. and M. Martin. 1980. *Teacher Expectations and Students Achievement—TESA*. Bloomington, Indiana: Phi Delta Kappan.

Koch, J. 1988. *AIDS: A Primer for Children*. Roslyn, NY: Berrent Publications Inc.

Lord, J. H. 1990. *Death at School: A Guide for Teachers, School Nurses, Counselors, and Administrators*. Dallas: Mothers Against Drunk Driving (M.A.D.D.).

Matter, D. E. and M. M. Roxana. 1989. "If Beautiful Is Good Then Ugly Must Be . . .: Confronting Discrimination Against the Physically Unattractive Child," *Elementary School Guidance and Counseling*, 24:2.

McCune, S. D. 1986. *Guide to Strategic Planning for Educators*. Alexandria, Virginia: Association for Supervision and Curriculum Development.

McPartland, J. M. and R. E. Slavin. 1990. *Increasing Achievement of At-Risk Students at Each Grade Level*. Policy Perspective, Office of Educational Research and Information, US Department of Education.

Mitchell, R. 1989. "Off the Tracks," *Perspective*, 1(3):1−16.

Morine-Dershimer, G. 1983. "Instructional Strategy and the Creation of Classroom Status," *American Educational Research Journal*, 20(4):645−661.

National School Boards Association. 1988. *First Teachers: Parental Involvement in the Public Schools*. Alexandria, Virginia.

National School Boards Association. 1989. *An Equal Chance: Educating At-Risk Children to Succeed*. Alexandria, Virginia.

Natriello, G., ed. 1987. *School Dropouts: Patterns and Policies*. New York: Columbia University Teachers College Prep.

Natriello, G., A. M. Pallas, E. L. McDill, J. M. McPartland, and D. Royster. 1988. *An Examination of the Assumptions and Evidence for Alternative Dropout Prevention Programs in High School. Report No. 365*. Baltimore, Maryland: Center for Social Organizations of Schools, The Johns Hopkins University.

New Jersey School Boards Association. 1990. *Dropout Prevention: A Resource Guide*. Trenton, New Jersey: Educational Horizons Series.

Newmann, F. M. 1981. "Reducing Student Alienation in High Schools: Implications of Theory," *Harvard Educational Review,* 51(4):546−564.

Oakes, J. *Keeping Track: How Schools Structure Inequality*. New Haven, Connecticut: Yale University.

Ogden, E. H. and V. Germinario. 1988. *The At-Risk Student: Answers for Educators*. Lancaster, PA: Technomic Publishing Co., Inc.

O'Gorman, P. 1981. *Teaching about Alcohol*. New York: Allen & Bakin.

Olweus, D. 1984. "Aggressors and Their Victims: Bullying at School," in *Disruptive Behavior in the Schools,* N. Frude and H. Gault, eds., New York: Wiley, pp. 57−76.

Pallas, A., G. Natriello, and E. McDill. 1989. "The Changing Nature of the Disadvantaged Generation: Current Dimensions and Future Trends," *Educational Researcher*, 18:16−22.

Patzer, G. 1983. "Source Credibility as a Function of Communicator Physical Attractiveness," *Journal of Business Research*, 11:229−241.

Perkins, H. 1965. "Classroom Behavior and Underachievement," *American Educational Research Journal*, 2:1−11.

Pfeffer, C., H. R. Conte, R. Plutchik, and I. Jerrett. 1979. "Suicidal Behavior in Latency Age Children: An Empirical Study," *Journal of American Academy of Child Psychiatry*, 18:679−692.

Phlegar, J. M. 1987. *Good Beginnings for Young Children: Early Identification of High Risk Youth and Programs that Promote Success*. Andover, Massachusetts: Northeast Regional Educational Laboratory.

Pogrow, S. 1988. "HOTS: A Thinking Skills Program for At-Risk Students," *Young Children*, 43(4):19−23.

Purkey, S. and M. Smith. 1983. "Effective Schools: A Review," *The Elementary School Journal*, 83(4):427−452.

Ragouzeos, B. 1987. *The Grieving Student in the Classroom*. Lancaster, Pennsylvania: Hospice of Lancaster County.

Rest, R. C. 1970. "Students Social Class and Teacher Expectations: The Self-Fulfilling Prophecy in Ghetto Education," *Harvard Educational Review,* 40(August):411−451.

Richman, L. 1978. "The Effects of Facial Disfigurement on Teacher's Perceptions of Ability in Cleft Palate Children," *Cleft Palate Journal,* 15:155−160.

Roberts, Fitzmahon and Associates. 1986. *Here's Looking at You 2000.* Seattle, Washington: Educational Services District #121.

Shepard L. and M. Smith. 1989. *Flunking Grades: Research and Policies on Retention.* London: Falmer Press.

Slavin, R. E. 1991. "Synthesis of Research on Cooperative Learning," *Educational Leadership,* 48(5):71−82.

Slavin, R. E. and N. A. Madden. 1989. *Effective Program for Students at Risk.* Boston: Allyn and Bacon.

Slavin, R. E. and N. A. Madden. 1989. "What Works for Students at Risk: A Research Synthesis," *Educational Leadership*, 46(5):4−13.

Smith, G. 1985. "Facial and Full-Length Ratings of Attractiveness and Friendliness in Interpersonal Attraction," *Sex Roles*, 12:287−293.

Stallings, J. 1980. "Allocated Academic Learning Time Revisited, or Beyond Time on Task," *Educational Researcher*, 9(11):11−16.

Stefanowski-Harding, S. 1990. "Suicide and the School Counselor," *The School Counselor*, 37:328−336.

Strother, D. B. 1983. "Practical Applications of Research: Mental Health Education," *Phi Delta Kappan*, 65(2):140−141.

US Center of Educational Statistics. 1989. *Dropout Rates in the United States.*

US Department of Education. 1990. *A Profile of the American Eighth Grader.* Office of Educational Research and Improvement, National Education Longitudinal Study of 1988.

US Department of Health, Education and Welfare. 1989. *The Educator's Role in the Prevention and Treatment of Child Abuse and Neglect.* Washington, DC: US Government Printing Office.

US Department of Health and Human Services. 1988. *Understanding AIDS.* Rockville, Maryland: Centers for Disease Control.

Wehlage, G. G. and R. Ritter. 1986. "Dropping Out: How Much Do Schools Contribute to the Problem?" *Teacher College Record,* 87(3).

Wheelock, A. and G. Dirman. 1988. *Before It's Too Late: Dropout Prevention in the Middle Grades.* Boston, Massachusetts: Center for Early Adolescence and Massachusetts Advocacy Center.

Will, M. C. 1986. "Educating Children with Learning Problems: A Shared Responsibility," *Exceptional Children*, 52(5).

EVELYN HUNT OGDEN received her Ed.D. from Rutgers University in Educational and Psychological Measurement and Statistics. She is the author of major studies and reports on effective and ineffective schools, programs that work, strategies to increase student achievement, reduce school violence, and disseminate successful practices in education. She is coauthor of *The At-Risk Student: Answers for Educators*, which dealt with at-risk students from a K−12 perspective. She currently serves on the U.S. Department of Education panel that reviews the effectiveness of educational programs and the panel that selects elementary schools for national recognition as Blue Ribbon Schools of Excellence. Her twenty-five years of administrative experience in education have included roles as Deputy Assistant Commissioner for Research, Planning and Evaluation, New Jersey Department of Education; Director of Assistance to the National Diffusion Network (NDN); Director of Curriculum, Moorestown, New Jersey; and her current position as Deputy Superintendent, East Brunswick, New Jersey.

VITO GERMINARIO received his Ed.D. from Rutgers University in Educational Administration and Supervision. He has teaching experience at the junior high, high school, and university levels. Dr. Germinario has been an elementary and middle school principal and an Assistant Superintendent. Currently, Dr. Germinario serves as Superintendent of the Moorestown Township Public Schools. Dr. Germinario lectures and conducts workshops for numerous schools throughout the nation and for professional organizations such as the Association for Supervision and Curriculum Development, National Association for School Executives, and National Association of Student Assistance Professionals. Dr. Germinario has published several articles for nationally known journals and most recently has coauthored a book entitled, *The At-Risk Student: Answers for Educators*.

JANET CERVALLI is a certified school psychologist who is currently pursuing a Ph.D. at Seton Hall University in Child Clinical Psychology. She has provided intervention services for high-risk youth within the general education population as well as within an alternative program that she coordinated for an urban school district. Ms. Cervalli serves as a trainer/consultant in the areas of crisis intervention, peer programs, student assistance, and supervision of counseling personnel for school districts throughout the state of New Jersey. She assists the New Jersey Department of Education in preparing new student assistance teams in the development of their programs. Ms. Cervalli is presently employed as the Supervisor of the Guidance, Health, and Student Assistance programs for the East Brunswick Public Schools in New Jersey.